LE CONFLIT EUROPÉEN EN 1914
Les voilà, les deux qui voulaient dévorer l'Europe

to George & Bozena
My Good Friends and Neighbors
With All My Best Wishes

Stephan Ikosky
1- March- 2017

I know you're neither George
nor Bozena, but at least you
can read the author's hand
writing

03/22/2020

WITH A WEAPON AND A GRIN

C'est le blanc qui crée le nègre.
— *Frantz Fanon*

WITH A WEAPON AND A GRIN:

Postcard Images of France's Black African Colonial Troops in WWI

Stephan Likosky

REPRESENTANTES DE LAS NACIONES ALIADAS QUE QUIEREN ANIQUILAR ALEMANIA Y AUSTRIA - HUNGRIA
CENTROS DE LA CULTURA Y DE LA CIVILIZACIÓN MODERNA

LOS REPRESENTANTES DE LA *CULTURA* Y DE LA *CIVILIZACION* CONTRA LOS *BARBAROS* ALEMANES Y AUSTRIACOS
ESCENA DEL CAMPO DE PRISIONEROS EN DÖBERITZ CERCA DE BERLÍN

Schiffer Publishing Ltd®

4880 Lower Valley Road • Atglen, PA 19310

Designed by RoS
Cover design by Molly Shields
Type set in LettrGoth12 BT/Utopia Std

ISBN: 978-0-7643-5227-0
Printed in China

Published by Schiffer Publishing, Ltd.
4880 Lower Valley Road
Atglen, PA 19310
Phone: (610) 593-1777; Fax: (610) 593-2002
E-mail: Info@schifferbooks.com
Web: www.schifferbooks.com

For our complete selection of fine books on this and related subjects, please visit our website at www.schifferbooks.com. You may also write for a free catalog.

Schiffer Publishing's titles are available at special discounts for bulk purchases for sales promotions or premiums. Special editions, including personalized covers, corporate imprints, and excerpts, can be created in large quantities for special needs. For more information, contact the publisher.

We are always looking for people to write books on new and related subjects. If you have an idea for a book, please contact us at proposals@schifferbooks.com.

CONTENTS

ACKNOWLEDGMENTS

I would like to thank Dan Miranda for helping instill in me his infectious love and appreciation of postcards and demonstrating to me that each and every card has a legend, history, and special meaning all its own and worthy of attention. I would also like to express my appreciation to Alan Petrulis of MetroPostcard.com for encouraging me in my writing and sharing with me some of his vast knowledge and understanding of WWI postcards. Many thanks also to Ian Robertson, my editor at Schiffer Publishing, and Jamie Elfrank, Marketing Manager, for their help and support.

INTRODUCTION

Early postcards are invaluable in providing us with a window to the past through which we can better understand the present. The purpose of *With a Weapon and a Grin* is to examine the images of France's black African soldiers in WWI and demonstrate the important role postcards played in the creation and manipulation of these images to further the propaganda efforts of the war's protagonists.

Though there are countless studies of WWI, there is surprisingly little material available in English on France's deployment of its African troops in Europe. Even more difficult to find is any examination of the black African soldier's pictorial image, especially as reflected on postcards contemporary to the time. It is my hope to address this gap and shed light on a long-neglected aspect of the Great War.

The importance of the postcard cannot be overestimated. During its golden age (1898–1919), billions of cards were printed and exchanged throughout the world. In 1909, an estimated 833 million cards were mailed in Great Britain, 668 million in the United States, 160 million in Germany, and 18 million in France.[1] This was a time when the cinema was at its beginnings, tourist travel for most was unaffordable, and photography was still in the early stages of adaptation for the news media. The postcard was a primary means by which the ordinary person was exposed to images of the world beyond his or her daily experiences.

Among their many functions, postcards were used for everyday communication, courting, as souvenirs for travelers, for advertising products and services and, when converted from photographs, as family mementoes to be shared. They were produced to celebrate, commemorate, and document a wide array of events, from family get-togethers to devastating floods, battle scenes, world's fairs, or simply birthdays and holidays. With the outbreak of WWI, the importance of postcards for propagandistic purposes took on monumental importance: entire nations needed to become mobilized and passions aroused. The "we versus them" cast of mind, the unquestioned support for one's own troops, and the demonization of the enemy would have to be instilled in the population and sustained until victory. What better weapon than the postcard: inexpensive to purchase and mail, durable, easily portable, and able to convey an image and written message.

Interestingly, the images reflected on postcards used for propaganda often reveal far less of the subjects themselves than of the entities producing such images. For example, when conquering Africa was a primary goal for France, it was expedient to show the African as a savage in need of civilizing. When African troops were needed in Europe to help in the war against Germany, this predominant image suddenly changed to a courageous soldier assimilable to French culture, sporting a big smile, loyal to the motherland, and non-threatening to French civilians. Paradoxically, France would continue to exploit the image of the black African soldier as part savage once it realized its potential to terrorize enemy troops. In all cases, the images of the African were being created and manipulated to reflect the changing needs of the image maker.

Postcards also reflect the various means by which Europeans projected some of their innermost fears and anxieties on to "the other." The threat of the African male to white women when tens of thousands of African troops were stationed in Europe during WWI was a common perception, though treated in significantly different ways by the French and Germans. The French refashioned his image from that of a primitive to a desexualized and childlike caricature, while the Germans portrayed him relentlessly as a savage, with the potential to racially pollute civilized nations.

To better understand the antique postcard we need to consider it in historical context, and hold in abeyance some of our contemporary notions which may prejudice us. The categorization of peoples into stages of development, for example, was regarded as science in the late nineteenth and early twentieth centuries. For blacks at the time, it constituted a step forward from the previous understanding of them as the inheritors of Ham's curse, forever destined to serve as slaves. Now the possibility was opened for the primitive or savage to evolve toward, if not attain, a European level of civilization. This was indeed the stated goal of France's *mission civilisatrice* (civilizing mission). Meanwhile, whereas today the use of the term "race" to categorize people based on physical features has lost its scientific validity, at the time of WWI, the term was still used as such, and was often interchangeable with "nation" or ethnic grouping.

Vocabulary can also be problematic. For Africans—until interacting with the Europeans—their primary identification was with their tribal group, i.e., Bambara or Tukulor. "Black" was not a name they called themselves, and they initially disapproved of being designated such by Europeans. By the onset of WWI, sub-Saharan Africans were already being grouped together as a race as "Negroes." For the French, the word *nègre*—ubiquitous on the early postcard—was not necessarily a derogatory term as it is today, though the term *sale nègre*—best translated as "dirty Nigger"—was a commonly used pejorative. Realizing the black troops heard *sale nègre* whenever *nègre* was used, a French training manual forbade its use and noted the Africans did not mind being called *noirs*.[2] The French word *sauvage*, depending on context, could indicate a person untainted by civilization and close to nature, as well as signifying "barbarian." Germans generally referred to all of France's darker-skinned colonial forces—North African as well as sub-Saharan—as "Blacks" (*Schwarze*). "Colored" (*Farbige*) and "Negroes" (*Neger*) were other common designations.

Petit nègre—a highly simplified and distorted form of French taught to the majority of African soldiers by the military—will be referred to frequently in this work. It was a language unique to WWI, and it served, one might argue, to infantize the troops and exert better control over them by limiting their interactions with the French. On postcards it is employed ubiquitously as the language of the black African troops, usually for humorous effect. In actuality, there were black soldiers, such as the *originaires* (see chapter 1), who did speak standard French, or were taught it in the army, while lower ranking black troops were sometimes tutored standard French by sympathetic civilians.[3]

I have limited my inclusion of cards to those I have acquired as an amateur collector. Sources over the years have included flea markets, postcard clubs, and Internet sales. The focus will be on the *tirailleurs sénégalais* (Senegalese infantrymen), the majority of France's sub-Saharan troops that fought in Europe. Since many North Africans were singled out due to their darker skin and were often referred to as "black," their images will also be included where relevant. In practice, names for the dark-skinned troops varied; one can find at times terms such as "Noirs," "Soudanais," "Armée Noire," "Turcos," and "Zouaves," as well as "Sénégalais," used interchangeably. While the time frame of this work encompasses WWI (1914–1918), the occupation of German territory by the French in the immediate aftermath of the fighting is included, given its relevancy to the major themes of my argument.

My hope is the reader will come away with a heightened interest in postcard collecting, as well as in the history and visual representation of the tirailleurs sénégalais. Though alternative forms of communication such as e-mail, texting, and Instagram have contributed to the rapidly diminishing importance of postcards, there is renewed interest in them as historic documents and for their artistic merit. A growing number of recent publications focusing on the vintage postcard, as well as the inclusion of cards in museum and gallery exhibits, testify to this phenomenon. Postcards are now highly sought by libraries, museums, specialized archives, artists, photographers, sociologists, and historians. I hope to demonstrate the collecting and study of postcards can offer us valuable insight toward a more balanced account of history, in this case the story of France's black African troops in WWI.

The book is divided into seven chapters, each with an overall focus on one or more stereotypical images of the French black African soldier. Chapter 1, Raw Recruit, offers the background and context for France's use of African forces on the battlefields of Europe. In chapter 2, Brave and Loyal Fighter, the heroic images of its African troops reflect France's attempt to justify and find popular acceptance for their employment in Europe, while Wounded Warrior (chapter 3) emphasizes the sacrifices black troops were making in defense of their mother country. In chapter 4, Grand Enfant, black soldiers are presented as gentle and naïve figures; children at heart who pose no threat to France's civilian population. Images in chapter 5, Semisavages, reflect France's decision to promote the African soldier as savage to exploit German fears, while at the same time continuing to depict him as a product of her civilizing mission. In chapter 6, Exotic Cannibal, German perspectives on France's African soldiers show them not only as cannibals, but as exotic creatures, at times even sympathetic as propagandistic goals shift. In Legacies (chapter 7), an exploration is made into some of the more lasting legacies of the war and how the nature of civilized behavior, indeed civilization itself, was called into question.

CHAPTER 1

RAW RECRUIT

The use of colonial troops by the French has a long history. As early as the Crimean War (1854–1856), almost half the French army was of African origin, and Africans also fought with the French in Mexico in the 1860s. In fact, the conquering of Africa was heavily contingent on the use of native soldiers.

In 1857, Napoleon III created an African Corps called the tirailleurs sénégalais, or Senegalese Infantrymen. In spite of the name, many of the men came not only from Senegal, but from Upper Volta, Guinea, and Mali. Other African colonial contingents included Algerians, Tunisians, Moroccans, and Malgaches from Madagascar. It was in Morocco in 1906, where the tirailleurs sénégalais aided French forces in suppressing anti-colonial rebellions, that the French military first saw the possibility for deployment of black soldiers in France. Col. Charles Mangin was its chief proponent. In 1910, in preparation for possible war with Germany, he wrote *La Force Noire*, in which he argued the black African recruit had natural abilities that suited him for soldiery: he was able to live in harsh climates; he was able to bear heavy loads over large distances; he had a less developed nervous system that resulted in a higher tolerance for pain; he was more apt to be obedient due to the strong patriarchal nature of his society; and he came from a continent where warfare was almost second nature. At the same time Mangin ranked various African tribes according to their skills and adaptability for service in a European war.[1]

Between 1914 and 1918, with Mangin's support, over 140,000 West Africans were recruited into the French Army and served as combatants on the Western Front. Of these, approximately 31,000 gave their lives.[2] The soldiers coming from Senegal were divided into two groupings, the originaires and the tirailleurs. The originaires were men from the communes of St. Louis, Gorée, Rufisque, and Dakar who enjoyed some rights of French citizenship, such as the ability to vote and access to the French legal system. During the war, they were integrated directly into French units and enjoyed certain privileges, such as furloughs that were less restrictive than those granted ordinary tirailleurs. On postcards, tirailleurs is the generic term for both these groupings, and for purposes of this survey no distinction will be made.

Before WWI, European encounters with Africans were limited mostly to world fairs and exhibitions, where indigenous peoples were put on display—not unlike exotic animals—to be goggled at by visitors. In spite of attempts by French officials to allay fears by isolating African troops from civilian contact, assigning them mostly to segregated units, and instructing them in the minimal amount of French necessary to perform their duties, the Great War would present the opportunity for ordinary French civilians to interface with Africans directly and on an unprecedented large scale. Propaganda would help reassure the French that the African savage was now a disciplined soldier willing to serve his mother country. At the same time, his image would be softened to show a less threatening side: he was now a naïve and child-like figure—a *grand enfant*—amicable and ever ready to flash a broad smile.

Along with the exploration and colonization of Africa, Social Darwinism and early anthropology played important roles in the construct of Africa and its inhabitants. The scientific classification of new fauna, flora, and inhabitants of countries being explored became almost a national passion in England, France, and Germany. Social Darwinists and anthropologists were largely responsible for the notion of stages of civilization into which the world's peoples could be placed. A German card (Fig. 1-01) shows the world's five races, with the centered Caucasian male epitomizing the highest level.

Fig. 1-01

MISSIONS des P. P. du SAINT-ESPRIT
Sacrifice païen – On consulte les augures

Fig. 1-02

Most early images of Africans circulated on European and American postcards portrayed them as savages in need of civilizing or slaves in need of liberation. These images were perfectly suited to help justify Europe's incursions into Africa and subsequent exploitation of the continent. On a missionary card (Fig. 1-02), two men are shown consulting the augurs as part of a "pagan sacrifice."

Fig. 1-03

AFRICA ANGOLA— SECURED BY NIGHT AND MARCHED BY DAY, UNTIL DELIVERED TO A PURCHASER. (AN ILLUSTRATION)

Fig. 1-03

48 A Christian Home and a Heathen Hut, Ikoko, Africa. (AMERICAN BAPTIST MISSIONARY UNION, BOSTON)

Fig. 1-04

A sympathetic portrayal of a bound slave appears on card 1-03. Its caption reads in part: "Secured by night and marched by day until delivered to a purchaser." In Fig. 1-04—a missionary "before and after" card—two families are shown. The image to the left points to the primitive nature of the African before the benefits of Christian civilization; barefooted and semi-naked figures stand outside their ramshackle hut. The right side of the card depicts a Christianized family, wherein all figures are modestly dressed in keeping with Western mores, and their hut is well-constructed. Even the tree behind their abode is manipulated to appear sturdier and healthier.

The exhibition of native peoples on the European continent at world's fairs and expositions reinforced popular images of Africans as less civilized members of the human race. They were people to be observed for the edification of the visitor and at the same time provided a source of amusement. The "we vs. them" dynamic was fully evident. "We" was commonly understood as the civilized European and "them" symbolized those trapped by race and biological determinism on the lower rungs of civilization.[3] Ethnic villages abounded at fairs and exhibitions from 1890 to 1931. In France alone—excluding Paris—there were fifty-eight at exhibitions in forty-one cities during this period. They also made appearances in Saint Petersburg, Palermo, Milan, Prague, Oslo, Warsaw, Glasgow, Dublin, Barcelona, and innumerable cities in Germany. Across the Atlantic, ethnic villages were constructed at World Fairs in Chicago in 1893, Saint Louis in 1894 and 1904, San Francisco in 1894, and Buffalo in 1901.[4]

Exposition Universelle de Liége 1905.

Village Sénégalais. — Cordonnier.

Fig. 1-05

Within the African villages at international fairs and expos, the visitor would find examples of Africans pursuing their day-to-day activities. On card 1-05, "The Cobbler," well-dressed visitors at the Liège exhibition in 1905 can be seen ambling about an African cobbler's abode. Note the fence separating the African structure from the observers. Its purpose was to discourage the harassment of natives by whites, who might poke at them or invade whatever little privacy they might enjoy.

If international exhibitions claimed an educational component in their display of native peoples, this was not the case in many of the local fairs popular throughout Europe. On an illustrated Gruss (Greetings from) card (Fig. 1-06), fair visitors are shown expressing shock and morbid curiosity as they are titillated by Snow White asleep in a cage and the two horrifying scenes bordering it. On the left, a gorilla holds a helpless and struggling woman in his arms, while to the right, a threatening dark-skinned native stands with a club over the body of a passed out blonde woman with breasts partially bared. Aside from the card's lampooning of political figures like Chamberlain and Cecil Rhodes, the underlying message of the threat to the white woman posed by lust driven ape-like savages could not be clearer.

Fig. 1-06

13 CASABLANCA. — AU CAMP SÉNÉGALAIS : L'EXERCICE.
Édition spéciale des Magasins Modernes

Fig. 1-07

In Fig. 1-07, West African troops with their French commander are shown at a camp in Casablanca, Morocco. It was here that Col. Mangin first came upon the idea such soldiers could be deployed in France's European military campaigns.

By the start of WWI, close to 10,000 Senegalese troops were deployed in Morocco; it is here their reputation as a solid and resilient fighting force for the French took hold. Countless postcards were produced documenting the lives of these fighters. Many show them with their families, who were allowed to accompany them. However, the image of the tirailleur as a cartoon-like semi-savage figure also traces its origins to this period. On postcard 1-08, titled L'Armée Française au Maroc, a tirailleur holds his machete in one hand and the ears of an enemy combatant in the other. He remarks in petit nègre, "These Moroccan ears are nice, and they're good luck charms." Combined are all the elements and contradictions that will later define the African tirailleur in the popular mind of France. Though he is a uniformed soldier trained by and loyal to the French, and has killed an enemy fighter, he has nonetheless resorted to mutilation, remains barefoot, believes a decimated human body part can ward off harm, and speaks a simplistic version of French that would strike educated French speakers as sounding ridiculous.

L'Armée Française au Maroc

Ça y a bon zareilles Marocains. Y a gris gris

M. Kerambrun et P. Cousin, éditeurs, Rabat - Reproduction réservée

Fig. 1-08

POUR LE DROIT ET LA CIVILISATION

Le Gl Mangin

Fig. 1-09

LES TROUPES NOIRES A LA FRONTIÈRE
LE GENERAL MANGIN

Fig. 1-10

Fig. 1-09 is a patriotic portrayal of Gen. Mangin titled "For Law and Civilization." On card 1-10, Gen. Mangin sits with binoculars and his saber beside him while an African horseman stands guard in the background. The caption "Black troops at the border" reinforces his association with France's African colonial armies.

Fig. 1-11

Fig. 1-12

Fig. 1-11 shows the recruitment of West African men into French colonial forces. Following Mangin's advice, recruitment levels were increased sharply at the onset of WWI to support the needs of continental French forces. In an ad (Fig. 1-12) for a popular French aperitif, African soldiers are seen disembarking to the welcoming gestures of French white forces.

Senegalese troops usually set off from Dakar, Senegal, to the French port cities Marseille and Bordeaux. The voyage typically lasted eight to ten days.

The excitement and energy felt in the scene of the departing troops in figure 1-12 is absent on photo card Fig. 1-13, titled "On board. The call up of the Tirailleurs Sénégalais," postmarked 1914. Here, the faces of the African soldiers crowded aboard express uncertainty and even disgruntlement. The journey to France for the vast majority was harsh. Conditions were dismal, many of the passengers became ill, and their movement on board was severely restricted.

Fig. 1-13

Fig. 1-14

The arrival of French black African troops on metropolitan French soil is noted on postcard 1-14. A group of black soldiers stand with their commanders shortly after arriving in Marseille in 1913. The adjutants pictured include two of West African origin. The caption reads: "Our Colonial Troops in France – 14 July, 1913. The arrival of the tirailleurs sénégalais – Adjutants: Martineau, Mamaditararoie, Barkeldiallo."

On card 1-15, captioned "War 1914/ The arrival of the Tirailleurs Sénégalais in Marseille," young French boys—one beating on a makeshift drum—march along the street with the newly arrived African soldiers. Their excitement at seeing black men perhaps for the first time is palpable.

Fig. 1-15

Recently arrived tirailleurs sénégalais line up to board a train on postcard 1-16. It is 1914, in the early phases of the war, when the conflict can still be referred to as the "campaign of 1914."

Fig. 1-16

Fig. 1-17

In Fig. 1-17, the evolution from primitive tribesman to soldier is illustrated by a female symbol of France viewing the African troops as they emerge from their native villages to parade past a triumphal arch (Honor and Homeland) toward the Invalides, symbol of French military power. The translated caption reads: "To My Children of the Black Continent. France the One and Indivisible Protectrice." In bold letters on the verso can be found: "Encouragement for the Indigenous Soldier in France." The West African soldiers are now "children" of France, emerging en masse from the "Black Continent" under the caring eyes of a French protectress that symbolizes their freedom and advancement. How very proud and grateful these troops must be, the postcard implies. And now it is the duty of the French populace to accept them and give them support.

CHAPTER 2

BRAVE AND LOYAL FIGHTER

Once the "savagery" of the African has been channeled into military discipline in service to France, the tirailleur sénégalais's invincibility is practically assured. Innumerable postcard images depict him helping protect France against the barbarous Huns. He is typically tall and proud in stature and wears his trademark red chechia cap. His courage is shown in battle scenes ranging from Alsace to the Marne, where his skills in hand-to-hand combat and readiness to use his *coupe-coupe* (machete) were legendary. Oftentimes he is drawn cartoon-like—larger than life and heroically vanquishing the foe while brandishing the spiked helmets of the Germans he has captured or killed.

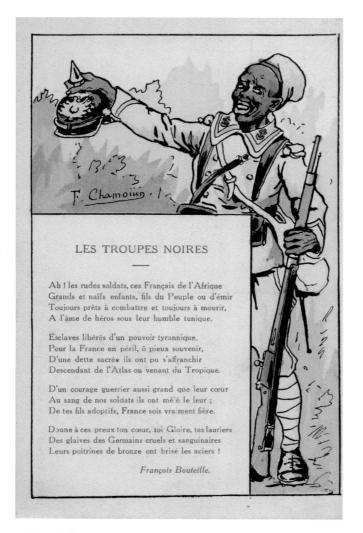

LES TROUPES NOIRES
—

Ah ! les rudes soldats, ces Français de l'Afrique
Grands et naïfs enfants, fils du Peuple ou d'émir
Toujours prêts à combattre et toujours à mourir,
A l'âme de héros sous leur humble tunique.

Esclaves libérés d'un pouvoir tyrannique,
Pour la France en péril, ô pieux souvenir,
D'une dette sacrée ils ont pu s'affranchir
Descendant de l'Atlas ou venant du Tropique.

D'un courage guerrier aussi grand que leur cœur
Au sang de nos soldats ils ont mê'é le leur ;
De tes fils adoptifs, France sois vraiment fière.

Donne à ces preux ton cœur, toi Gloire, tes lauriers
Des glaives des Germains cruels et sanguinaires
Leurs poitrines de bronze ont brisé les aciers !

François Bouteille.

Fig. 2-01

Tirailleurs Sénégalais

Fig. 2-02

In a poetic tribute to the black troops (Fig. 2-01), the African soldier is drawn with a smile on his face as he holds up the helmet of a German combatant. "These Frenchmen from Africa" we are told are "large and naive children" ready to fight and die for France. They are "liberated slaves" with a great courage that matches their hearts. France is truly proud of them. The postcard is able to capture the childlike qualities of the African while at the same time assuring us of his bravery when confronting the enemy. The civilizing mission of the French has elevated the African from enslavement on the Dark Continent to a defender of France in Europe. In Fig. 2-02, titled "tirailleurs sénégalais," we are presented with a tall and proud West African soldier in full uniform, his gear on his back and his bayonetted rifle by his side. His relaxed stance and hand in his pocket make for an approachable yet self-assured individual.

Fig. 2-03

It would be difficult to imagine a more compelling tribute to the Senegalese infantryman than that found in Fig. 2-03. The illustration is titled: "THE NEW MAGI KINGS. CHRISTMAS! These are truly the sons of the Magi Kings: the Senegalese, Indian, and the Arab offer their humble gifts to a Belgian child inside a farm in Flanders, where the ravages of war have left only a cow shed." Reference is to the German invasion and subjugation of Belgium, a neutral country at the beginning of WWI. Here, the Belgian victims—mother and child—are compared to Mary and Jesus, while the "New Magi Kings" represent the troops from the colonies uniting with the European soldiers gathered around to ward off the German enemy. The black African fighter is sympathetically drawn, kneeling directly in front of the child and tenderly presenting his gift.

In Fig. 2-04, a tirailleur sénégalais has captured Wilhelm II of Germany and Emperor Franz Joseph of Austria-Hungary. He holds the cringing figures in a choke-hold as he looks up proudly from his conquests. The caption reads: "The European Conflict in 1914. Here they are, the two who wanted to devour Europe." The African soldier is here regarded unambiguously as the savior of Europe. Card 2-05 recalls popular song lyrics that read: "One white woman is worth two black women (see Fig. 4-19)." Above an illustration of a "noir" leading four captured Germans toward Paris, this variant of the song's lyrics reads: "One Black man is worth four Boches." (Boche is a pejorative term for "German.") It is an interesting juxtaposition, countering the higher value placed on white women over black women with the black soldier's worth four times that of a German soldier.

LE CONFLIT EUROPEEN EN 1914
Les voilà, les deux qui voulaient dévorer l'Europe

Fig. 2-04

UNE BLANCHE VAUT 2 NOIRES

UN NOIR VAUT 4 BOCHES

Fig. 2-05

SÉRIE HUMORISTIQUE DE LA GUERRE 1914

Le Turco qui a tué 18 uhlans
— Qu'est-ce que tu fais-là ?
— Ma lieutenant, j'occupe le village.

28

Fig. 2-06

The celebration of a tirailleur's individual heroism is depicted on Fig. 2-06, titled "The Turco who killed 18 uhlans." The illustration shows a black soldier saluting two white officers who ask him: "What are you doing here?" The black soldier responds: "My lieutenant, I'm occupying the village." A large official car and horses fill the background. The scene refers to an actual incident in August 1914, when Gen. Mangin's motor escort was attacked by an eleven-man German patrol. Gen. Mangin—in charge of West African forces—had a loyal bodyguard, Baba Koulibaly, a six-foot-four-inch Bambara who in the end served him from 1903–1922. The bodyguard drove off the German patrol, then chased away a second patrol of six men, and after linking up with a group of French cavalry was able to repel yet another attack. Being a foot soldier, Koulibaly declined riding off with the cavalrymen, instead placing himself solidly in the middle of the town square. When later discovered and asked what he was doing there, the bodyguard replied he was occupying the village. This was a story Gen. Mangin liked to tell, and it became a well-circulated tale of bravery.[1] It is unique in its glorification of an actual African soldier, though Koulibaly's name does not appear on the card. Still, the story was known well enough to be understood by postcard viewers, scant as it is in background detail. As an interesting footnote, Gen. Mangin was said to have cut a dashing figure accompanied by his Senegalese bodyguard, taking daring risks in battle and traveling in the flaming red German 1914 Opel he captured that is depicted.

Gloire à la plus grande France
9387
— J·K —

Fig. 2-07

Gloire à la plus grande France
9387
— J·K —

Fig. 2-08

Three cards (Figs. 2-07 to 2-09) picture a boyish looking black soldier handling two German spiked helmets, presumably captured in battle. Holding them against his body, placing one atop his bayonet and then atop his head, he grins with a look of satisfaction. The caption "Glory to Greater France" lauds the French motherland as a multiracial colonial empire. The cards are three of five in a set.

Gloire à la plus grande France

9387

J.K.

Fig. 2-09

Cliché Chusseau-Flaviens

1914... EN BELGIQUE — Senegalais gardant
22me Série la voie entre Dixmude et Nieuport | **1914... IN BELGIUM** - Senegalése watching the railway between Dixmude and Nieuport

Fig. 2-10

En Alsace. — Tirailleurs sénégalais repoussant une attaque.

Fig. 2-11

One of the functions the tirailleurs sénégalais performed during the war was guard duty, especially on trains with enemy prisoners. In Fig. 2-10, the soldiers are patrolling a railway line in Belgium. Two stand along the rails, while at center left a soldier is sitting, cleaning his rifle. In Fig. 2-11, "In Alsace – tirailleurs sénégalais repulse an attack," the African troops are amassed in a trench-like ditch, with three soldiers taking up firing positions and two at the ready with hand grenades.

Guerre 1914 - Dans la Marne (*Nos Tirailleurs Sénégalais enlèvent les canons allemands*

Fig. 2-12

EN GUERRE.- BATAILLE DE LA MARNE.
LES TURCOS A GERMIGNY-L'ÉVÊQUE.

THE WAR.- THE BATTLE OF THE MARNE.
THE TURCOS AT GERMIGNY-L'ÉVÊQUE.

Fig. 2-13

The (First) Battle of the Marne was fought September 5–12, 1914, with French and British forces facing German troops. It was one of the first key battles of the war, and is said to have saved nearby Paris from falling into the hands of the enemy while assuring France's continuation as a combatant. Over two million soldiers fought in the battle, with over 500,000 killed or wounded.[2] In Fig. 2-12, tirailleurs sénégalais are shown capturing German cannons. The enemy soldiers have been overpowered and many lie dead on the field. A second battle scene from the Battle of the Marne (Fig. 2-13) depicts a forceful advance by African troops against a dramatic background of burning buildings. On the bottom left, a black soldier is bashing his rifle butt into a fallen German while another German soldier cowers in horror. Pictures like these served to bolster the argument early in the war for the use of African troops on the European battleground.

Fig. 2-14

Fig. 2-15

The illustration on Fig. 2-14 narrates an incident at the Battle of the Marne where German soldiers, in an attempt to hold their ground, purportedly erected a six and a half foot high barrier using the bodies of their dead and wounded soldiers. The French colonial forces broke through we are told, resulting in 7,000 enemy dead and a "fantastic" number of wounded. The German soldiers abandon their weapons as they flee.

A depiction of a nighttime confrontation at the Battle of the Aisne (Fig. 2-15) gives us a somewhat more realistic view of war, in that casualties are being suffered on both sides. Though African troops are overwhelming the Germans and the enemy machine gunner has abandoned his weapon, a Turco reels back after being shot. In the air above a reconnaissance plane has been spotted, and to the right an aerial explosion lights up the night. African troops are not only willing to die for the mother country but are actually doing so.

108. La Grande Guerre 1914-15 – La Garde Impériale défilant devant le Kaiser
Cette troupe orgueil de l'Allemagne fut anéantie par nos Turcos
à la Bataille de CHARLEROI   A. R.

Fig. 2-16

Card 2-16 does not portray colonial soldiers, but refers to them in an important piece of war propaganda. Its French caption reads: "The Great War 1914–1915 – The Imperial Guard parading before the Kaiser. This proud troop from Germany was annihilated by our Turcos at the Battle of CHARLEROI." Charleroi was fought early in the war on August 21, 1914, and ended in a decisive victory for the Germans. The colonial soldiers fought bravely for the French but suffered heavy losses. The card clearly distorts the outcome of this particular battle. A newspaper article at the time lauds the bravery of the African soldiers:

Paris Sept 2, 1914

"It was like hell cut loose," is the way a French officer of Zouaves described the charge of the Turcos, France's black troops at the Battle of Charleroi.

Telling of the terrific charges of the blacks, the officer declared, "they fought at such close quarters with the Germans that many of the men got hold of the noses of the enemy with their teeth. When the fighting was at the height our colonel suddenly ordered, 'give the Turcos free rein,'" said the officer... Then the avalanche began, it was like hell was set loose... When they were within fifteen yards of the batteries, the Germans had to cease firing to avoid shooting their own guards. A bloody bayonet fight then followed...The soldiers of the Kaiser were giants, but they fell like flies."[3]

The destruction of the German Imperial Guard is explicitly depicted on card 2-17, titled "Sénégalais Contre La Garde Impériale." In an intense and colorful scene, the French African troops are decimating their enemy. The caption below reads: "At the Battle of Charleroi, the Tirailleurs Sénégalais played a decisive role, with their fury, against the Imperial Guard, annihilating the enemy with bayonets. Prince Adalbert, the Kaiser's cousin, perished in the melee."

SÉNÉGALAIS CONTRE LA GARDE IMPÉRIALE   N. 5

A la bataille de Charleroi, les tirailleurs sénégalais tiennent un rôle prépondérant en donnant avec furie, au moment décisif, contre la garde impériale et en l'anéantissant à la baïonnette. Le prince Adalbert, cousin du Kaiser, périt dans la mélée.

Fig. 2-17

AT LAST..!

BIÈRE DE LA MEUSE

Fig. 2-18

On a French card (Fig. 2-18) captioned "AT LAST..!" in English, a French African soldier and an English soldier place a dead Kaiser Wilhelm into a coffin marked Bière de la Meuse (Meuse Beer). It refers to the battles along the Meuse River at the start of the war with the routing of the Germans by the Allies. Bières de la Meuse (Meuse Beers) were the theme for some of Alphonse Mucha's best known art nouveau poster ads. The northern Meuse region of France was indeed famous for its beers in contrast to most of France, where wines ruled supreme. That the armies of France are represented by a black African soldier emphasizes the importance France placed on its colonial forces.

Li pas peur, les Boches pire que lui.
Don't be afraid, the huns are worse.

Fig. 2-19

Le retour au Pays !
Non but the brave deserve the fair.

Fig. 2-20

Cartoon cards were a popular feature of postcard history during WWI. Especially prevalent in France, they provided humor and satire for trying times. In Fig. 2-19, a tirailleur sénégalais, his hands on his sword, looks up bravely at a lion while his woman friend is overcome with fright. The couple are shown diminutively in relation to the lion, rendering the animal all the more threatening. Both figures are barefoot, while the female is naked, except for a tricolor ribbon in her hair signifying France. The bravado of the soldier is countered by the reminder that he and his naked friend are primitives, one step removed from the jungle. The caption, in petit nègre and English, reads: "Don't be afraid, the Huns are worse."

On a companion card in the same series (Fig. 2-20), a tirailleur sénégalais stands proudly while his woman friend examines his badge for bravery. Again, she is near naked and wears the tricolor ribbon in her hair. The soldier carries a captured German spiked helmet as a souvenir from the war. The desert background with palms denotes an African setting.

CHAPTER 3

WOUNDED WARRIOR

In addition to the approximately 30,000 tirailleurs sénégalais who died fighting in the course of WWI, many thousands were wounded. This could not help but evoke sympathy and support in the eyes of the French for those fighting on their behalf. The nurse, meanwhile, became the symbol of female virtue in popular myth—sexually and morally pure, maternal, angelic, and sacrificing. Still, the nurses who tended to colonial soldiers were often suspected of coddling them, and this roused concern on the part of authorities as to their being confined together in such close quarters as hospitals and convalescent facilities. The nurses seemed to pay little attention to warnings not to fraternize or exchange photos with the African wounded. They were warned lest the soldiers share the photos with their compatriots, thereby demeaning white womanhood. At stake was a break in the social order of privileged white European males over women and colonized peoples.[1] Though fear of miscegenation led authorities in 1915 to establish segregated hospitals with male nurses for the Senegalese in the south of France, photo postcards abound depicting hospital wards with white nurses and black and white soldiers.

To defuse any hint of interracial sexual connections, the majority of postcards portray the black soldier as vulnerable and dependent beside the white nurse. He is confined to a bed or has his head or limbs bandaged. Where comic scenes of flirtation exist he is likely to be transformed into a desexualized and childlike creature. Many postcards do show the wounded tirailleur enjoying the admiring attention of attractive French women on city streets.

Fig. 3-01

Though nursing duties in France were traditionally performed by Catholic sisters, with the onset of the war, campaigns were mounted to enlist more women into the Red Cross and other charitable institutions to serve in hospitals and medical stations near the front. In Fig. 3-01, a nurse and a sister help a wounded soldier against a backdrop of a burning town. The caption reads: "Our wounded before and after, the burners of villages and killers of children."

The colonial soldier towers over the women, but the illustration focuses on the women's maternal and caring postures and the soldier's vulnerability.

1914... La lecture du Journal aux Blessés | 1914... The reading of the news-paper to the wounded

14me Série

Fig. 3-02

Against what seems a racially segregated setting (Fig. 3-02), a woman nurse reads the paper to a gathering of wounded colonial soldiers. Attempts by the French military to send wounded African soldiers to army hospitals with male nurses did not always succeed. Fig. 3-03 shows an integrated hospital setting with women nurses and French and black African wounded.

Fig. 3-03

Fig. 3-04

Pinx. M. Orange.   Croix Rouge et tête noir, deux cœurs d'or.   VISÉ PARI
                   Red cross and Black Head, two hearts of gold.   2342
M. Оранжъ.   Два золотыхъ сердца.   I. M. L.

Fig. 3-05

On a postcard (Fig. 3-04) written in 1916 titled La Bonne Nouvelle (Good News), a Red Cross nurse sits across the bed of a wounded tirailleur reading him his letter. The scene of a nurse sitting across a black soldier's bed might have raised eyebrows were it not for the soldier's sight impairment and his congenial and appreciative facial expression. The term "Good News" has religious significance, meaning salvation through Christ, and might be read into the card's message, especially as the white woman was seen as integral to France's civilizing mission.

A card published by the French Red Cross (Fig. 3-05) depicts a nurse looking up sympathetically at a wounded tirailleur on crutches. The caption in French and English reads: "Red Cross and Black Head, two hearts of gold"; in Russian, "Two gold hearts." The artful design and striking colors draw attention to and reinforce the notion of the wounded hero.

A highly stylized tribute to Red Cross nurses can be found on card 3-06. A nurse extends a helping hand to a smiling African soldier who is seated with his hand in bandages but still holding his weapon. The caption reads: "Hymn to France: France depends on them (the nurses). For them the duty is sweet."

Fig. 3-06

Fig. 3-07

In Fig. 3-07, another stylized depiction of a wounded tirailleur with a sister/nurse, a soldier sits with a bandaged right hand as a nurse leans tenderly toward him. There can be no doubt of the soldier's heroism as he holds in front of him a captured German helmet. The nurse helps hold the helmet, sharing with the soldier their common goal of German defeat. The caption reads: "Hymn to France: Our united hearts will carry you toward the heights of victory." The models for the young nurse and wounded boyish-looking soldier can be found on many cards.

IMPOSSIBLE SIDI QUE TU RETOURNES AU FEU TA LANGUE EST BLANCHE

Fig. 3-08

— Et vous mon ami,
avez-vous été blessé au front?
— Non, Madame, exactement au coté opposé.

— Moi content !...... bon tabac,
bons gâteaux, Zoulies femmes,
moi, toujours malade!

Fig. 3-09

The African soldier is treated satirically in Figs. 3-08 and 3-09. On card 3-08, a Red Cross nurse administers to a black patient who has his tongue stuck out. The nurse says: "Impossible, Sidi, that you return to the battlefront (as) your tongue is (still) white." A presumed ignorance on the part of the nurse is in perfect harmony with the wounded soldier's probable desire to not return to the front. The name Sidi is a generic term used by whites for Africans, though in Arabic it is a respectful title, meaning "my master."

Fig. 3-09 is a multi-paneled postcard. To the left, a woman visitor to a wounded white soldier asks him if he was wounded at the front. "No, Madam," he replies, "quite the opposite." Below, a battlefield scene shows the same soldier being hit by shrapnel in his derriere. On the right panel, a black wounded soldier lies in his hospital bed, being served by a white nurse. He smokes his pipe with a happy grin on his face. Below, in petit nègre, he exclaims: "I'm so happy! Good tobacco, good cakes, pretty women, I'm going to stay sick forever!" The childlike African has been seduced by the trappings of civilization.

Fig. 3-10

A similar grin is shared by the
wounded tirailleur sénégalais on card
3-10, titled "Good News."

A Red Cross nurse reads the paper
to her patient, whose black face stands
out against the white pillow and bedding.
The card was mailed in 1916, and the
sender has scribbled on the front: "Isn't
he a pretender – Our Sick One!!!"

Fig. 3-11

Fig. 3-12

In Fig. 3-11, two fashionably dressed young French women escort a wounded tirailleur with bandaged hand and cane along a city street. They look up at him in admiration while his face glows. Cards such as these were important in convincing the French that the African soldiers, risking their lives on the battlefield for France, presented no threat to the civilian population. In Fig. 3-12, two wounded soldiers— one a white Frenchman, the other a black African—walk together, attracting the admiration of a civilian couple. At the upper right, the French caption reads: "Our Heroes." The bold-faced caption in English at the bottom reads "Back From the battle," while directly below the two figures, the black soldier says to his friend in petit nègre: "You know, Fricot, this is good for the tirailleurs." Fricot is a French surname, and the card establishes a level of equality in the eyes of French civilian society between the black African and French white soldiers wounded in battle.

Fig. 3-13

A far less typical portrayal of the wounded black African solider and his nurse (Fig. 3-13) depicts a Red Cross nurse helping the tirailleur along with his cane and his arm in a sling. Here, the face of the solider, in spite of his smile, is leering, even a bit crazed, recalling some of the postcard figures of the African fighters in battle scenes. The caption reads "White sister and Black brother," sister having the double meaning of "sibling" and "nurse."

Fig. 3-14

A postcard in water colors (Fig. 3-14) shows a tirailleur with a wounded leg and cane walking down a Paris street with two fashionably dressed women. All three are fancifully transfigured into chickens. Using the stereotypical speech of an African tirailleur, the rooster comments: "Convalescence in Paris. I like it!!" The black African soldier is attracted to the beautiful white civilian women he sees. In reality, African soldiers were routinely sent to isolated camps or hospitals to recover, and not to France's major cities, to discourage interracial male-female encounters of this sort.

Fig. 3-15

A reminder the sacrifice of African troops for the cause of France should not be taken lightly is depicted with sarcasm on card 3-15. It is an illustration of a wounded tirailleur sénégalais holding out a captured German spiked helmet for sale to an older man in civilian clothes. Their interchange is as follows:

"Five francs for the helmet? That's (too) expensive!"
"Well, I can tell you where you can get the same thing for nothing..."
"And where's that?"
"On the battlefield!"

CHAPTER 4
GRAND ENFANT

Transforming the image of the "primitive" African male into one more palatable to the French populace was not an easy task. Starting in 1910, when Col. (later Gen.) Mangin suggested the use of black troops in the mother country, there was much public debate and concern over its appropriateness. Many French argued that Africans by nature were bloodthirsty and savage, and would inevitably present a danger, especially to French women. In response, French government officials deliberately set about to change this depiction of the African male to one who, though a fierce warrior, was naive and childlike by nature. Their campaign was helped immeasurably by the promotion of a popular banana-flavored chocolate drink called "Banania." Originally the breakfast drink pictured on its ad a woman from the Antilles, but in 1915, it was replaced by the image of a smiling and childlike tirailleur sénégalais. The accompanying expression on the ad, "Y'a bon"—petit nègre for "It's Good"—henceforth became strongly associated with the tirailleurs. The drink was distributed to French soldiers and the posters advertising it could be found all throughout France. A host of other postcards pictured the African troops going about their routines in ways making it easy for the viewer to identify: washing clothes, eating a meal, or relaxing outdoors. Of special interest were cards specifically meant to assure the French the tirailleur was non-threatening to their women and children. By today's standards they are almost comic in their patronizing stance.

Other real photo postcards show black and white soldiers fraternizing without the slightest hint of racial animus, while a subset—mostly illustrations and cartoon-like—acknowledge the African soldiers as sexual human beings. Like their white counterparts, they too frequented prostitutes and established correspondence with *marraines* (godmothers), civilian women who would undertake to write soldiers, send them socks, chocolate, tobacco, and even host them when they were on furlough. This comprised one of the more positive experiences African soldiers in France had with the civilian population, for the relationship between tirailleurs sénégalais and their French marraines often led to genuine friendships and a semblance of social equality. Tirailleur Mbaye Khary Diagne recalls the marraines:

> They were girls of good families who saw us and knew we were [far from] our countries. [And they realized] we needed some affection and some money...to buy cigarettes with, to go to the movies, and so on. [And we met them] on the street or in cafés. A French girl saw you and felt very pleased by [your appearance]. And she said to you that she wanted to take you to her house to present you to her parents. And you got [an adopted] French family in that way. [But] it wasn't necessary to have love affairs (with them). From time to time some marraines de guerre fell in love with the soldiers they invited home. But generally, they were only friendly relations.[1]

Fig. 4-01

Fig. 4-01 depicts the iconic image of the tirailleur sénégalais used in the ad for the breakfast drink Banania. The soldier sits with spoon uplifted and a broad smile on his face. Missing are the typically bulging eyes and exaggeratedly large lips often associated with the African in popular commercial ads. Though his rifle lies on the ground beside him, this is the relaxed, congenial figure long associated throughout France with the black African soldier.

Fig. 4-02

Fig. 4-03

On a card (Fig. 4-02) titled "The War 1914 – Tirailleurs Sénégalais – The Washbasin," soldiers are pictured washing themselves along a wall of washbasins. Soldiers washing their clothes in a river is the subject of card 4-03, titled "Silver Coast – Le Courneau – Senegalese camp – Wash house." Le Courneau was a camp in southwest France, facing the Atlantic. Along with Fréjus, Saint-Raphäel, and Oran (Algeria), it served as winter quarters (hivernage) for the African troops, who were having a difficult time adjusting to the harsh winters of Northern France. Over 40,000 African soldiers passed though the camp, which later in the war housed Russian, then American forces. Both cards, along with the two following, were meant to portray the African soldiers as "everyday" types, with habits and past-times no different than the ordinary soldiers.'

CROQUIS DE GUERRE
SEPTEMBRE 1914
Tirailleurs Sénégalais prenant leur repas

La C P A

Fig. 4-04

Fig. 4-05

In Fig. 4-04, a group of African soldiers are seated around a pot of food at mealtime. The photograph is somewhat reminiscent of those taken of Africans eating under the gawking stares of visitors at the world exhibitions, where native peoples were put on display as primitive creatures. Here it is the "ordinariness" of the act and not its exoticness that is emphasized. In 4-05, an amateur photographer has captured a group of Senegalese soldiers relaxing along the water.

Among the many postcards serving to allay the fears of the French regarding the African troops' presence in their midst, some focused more specifically on the country's women and children.

1914... Vendangeuse offrant du raisin
17me Série   a un blessé Sénégalais

1914... Grape-gatherer offering grapes
to a wounded senegal soldier

Fig. 4-06

On image 4-06, a French grape picker offers grapes to a wounded tirailleur sénégalais. Two women are shown by themselves in a vineyard as a large group of black soldiers comes marching by. The grape picker shows what can only be described as kindness and compassion to the soldier that has been wounded in service to France. The caption in French and English reads: "1914 – Grape-gatherer offering grapes to a wounded Senegalese soldier."

11 A Charente-Infre — Les Tirailleurs Malgaches à LA TREMBLADE en 1917
Sur cette Carte, nous voyons le tirailleur de gauche Raberanto et celui de droite Rabotojamaria, fraterniser avec les petits
Trembladais qui font bon ménage avec eux, les Malgaches n'étant pas dénués d'affection

Fig. 4-07

Figs. 4-07 and 4-08 depict black soldiers from Madagascar engaged with white French children. They belong to a series from La Tremblade, France, dated 1917. On the first, the caption reads: "On this card we see on the left Roberanto and on the right Robotojamaria, fraternizing with young Tremladians, who are getting along well with them, the Malgaches not being void of affection." Pictured are two African soldiers standing with their arms on the shoulders of four young French boys. What is exceptional is the black soldiers are named, whereas the French children are not. Standard practice was almost always to render black troops anonymous or, more generally, colonized types (i.e., tirailleurs sénégalais or type Malgache), instead of individualizing them with actual names. The propaganda value of the card is to assure the French populace that African soldiers arriving on their shores are not only non-threatening, but even capable of human affection.

The second card (Fig. 4-08) serves the same purpose, posing two male Madagascan volunteer nurses holding the hands of a young French girl standing on a chair between them. The caption reads: "Two Malgache tirailleurs, volunteer nurses. To the left, Razafimandinby, to the right, Talata. The two Malgaches are on duty. See the tenderness they show for the young French girl, to whom they affectionately give their hand." Bottom line: "French people, have no fear! The black Africans now serving our country present no harm to you or your children. In fact, they are quite capable of showing tenderness and affection."

12 Charente-Infre - Les Tirailleurs Malgaches à LA TREMBLADE en 1917
Les deux tirailleurs malgaches infirmiers de la 4e Cie, 13e Bne et engagés volontaires. A gauche,
Razafimandinby; à droite, Talata. Ces deux Malgaches sont bien à leur place au poste d'infirmiers;
voyez leur tendresse pour la petite Française, à qui ils donnent affectueusement la main.

Fig. 4-08

On a real photo postcard (Fig. 4-09) conveying a similar message to the two above, but neither patronizing in its approach nor explicitly propagandistic, a white boy leans against a seated black soldier whose hand holds the child around his waist. The boy looks toward the camera with self-confidence, while the soldier seems relaxed and content.

Fig. 4-09

One photo postcard documenting the amiability of French civilians and African military figures is dated May 20, 1916, from the French town Paray le Monial (Fig. 4-10), and is truly captivating. Thirty-five persons and a pet dog are featured. Male and female, black and white, adult and child, and military and civilian figures are all included. The photo is taken in front of a troop train transporting tirailleurs sénégalais. The woman and children show no discomfort; indeed, the scene is one of relaxed camaraderie. Of special note is the white French and black African soldier couple to the left of center, standing with their arms about each other. On postcard 4-11, a group of soldiers—both black and white—and a woman with her child pose for the camera. The mood is jovial and the affection reads as genuine.[2]

Even though the image of the tirailleur sénégalais was often desexualized by his being made childlike, postcards do exist that acknowledge him as a sexual being. Most appear as illustrations and are light-hearted. In this way, the tirailleur becomes more multidimensional without being seen as threatening.

Fig. 4-10

Fig. 4-11

Fig. 4-12

Artist A. Guillaume depicts a street scene (Fig. 4-12) in which a fashionable young woman is being admired by a number of military men. One is a smiling tirailleur with his cap tilted to the side. Regardless of race or ethnic origin, the men are all equal in their appreciation of a beautiful woman.

Fig. 4-13

Fig. 4-14

 Tactics limiting the closeness of an interracial relationship can be subtle. As an example, each in a set of four postcards representing the suits of a deck (hearts, spades, clubs, and diamonds) shows a uniformed soldier with an attractive woman (Figs. 4-13 to 4-16). Seen isolated, the card of diamonds with its tirailleur sénégalais presents a black African soldier seemingly on equal par with a white French woman. Perhaps he is regaling her with war stories as she looks at him admiringly. This is the only card in the series in which the woman is in no physical contact with the soldier. It is in sharp contrast to the card of hearts, where the poilu *is in close embrace with the white woman.*

Fig. 4-15

Fig. 4-16

Fig. 4-17

Artist "Griff"—creator of many cards with anthropomorphic rabbits—has given us (Fig. 4-17) a black tirailleur wooing a white female. Below the name of the card's series Nos Lapins (Our Rabbits) is the caption in petit nègre: "After the war, I'll take you back to Senegal and we'll have many little 'cafés au laits.'" The word lapin in French slang during WWI meant "a determined or cunning person." Café au lait is the name for French coffee with milk, but in slang it designates a person of mixed black and white heritage.

Fig. 4-18

A water color (Fig. 4-18) belonging to the same series as Fig. 3-14 shows two tirailleurs sénégalais and a white French soldier all portrayed as chickens looking up at a monument dedicated to the glory of the French Republic, which is symbolized by a woman. A black soldier points to the statue and says in petit nègre: "You see, the beautiful Republic, not white like your women, but like a Senegalese woman." To his way of seeing, an African woman is every bit as valued representing French ideals as a French white woman, the irony being in his interpretation of the metallic green as non-white, thus black.

Fig. 4-19

Fig. 4-20

Fig. 4-19 is more on the risqué side. Its title is "Music of the Bedroom," and it shows a series of female figures and soldiers with reference to popular songs. Most noteworthy is madelon, *referring to a widely circulating WWI song about soldiers flirting with a waitress in a rural tavern. As opposed to most soldiers' songs, this one had clean lyrics and was later turned into a patriotic song revived in WWII and sung by Marlene Dietrich. The English title was "I'll be true to the whole regiment." On the lower left, two black male figures, one identifiable as a tirailleur sénégalais, stand on either side of a seated woman with her undergarments exposed and hiding her face in shame. The translated caption reads: "One White Woman is Worth Two Black Women." On Fig. 4-20, a hand painted postcard with its caption in petit nègre curiously mixed with English (Y a good), a seemingly bare breasted young white woman turns flirtatiously toward a light skinned tirailleur with his refined (read: non-Negroid) features and smile. The card is decorative and light in spirit.*

Fig. 4-21

Xavier Sager (1870–1930) was a prolific illustrator of French postcards whose recurring motifs are social satire, eroticism, and Paris nightlife. In La sieste (The Siesta, Fig. 4-21), a woman is asleep stretched out on a chair, her feet resting on a table. Seated on her lap is a miniature tirailleur sénégalais with his hand touching the fringe of her undergarments and upper leg. Is this the white woman's fantasy of interracial love? Why is the black figure miniaturized? The picture is open to multiple interpretations.

Des goûts et des couleurs!...
Tastes and Colours always differ.

Fig. 4-22

MARSEILLE. - Rue Lantermery, près le vieux Port

Fig. 4-23

Fig. 4-22 depicts two interracial couples courting in a desert setting. The title, "Tastes and Colours Always Differ" (Des goûts et des couleurs!), hints at open tolerance made more palatable by use of cartoon stereotypes. Yet, in spite of this, the black male figure—a uniformed tirailleur sénégalais— remains barefoot, a long-standing symbol of African savagery, and the white French officer in colonial garb walks with an indigenous woman wearing little more than a ribbon.

While serving in France's earlier Moroccan campaigns, the tirailleurs sénégalais were allowed to live with their families, a privilege discontinued as being too costly in Europe. One consequence was African soldiers, as their white counterparts, often resorted to prostitution to fulfill their sexual needs. Titled "Marseille – Lantermery St., near the old port," a 1918 photo postcard (Fig. 4-23) shows a group of prostitutes in Marseille posing for the camera along with potential customers, including a tirailleur sénégalais. Photo postcards such as this were more likely to capture some of the realities of the tirailleur's experiences in France than the more commercially produced and mass distributed illustrated cards.

Fig. 4-24

Ma jolie Marraine, j'ai un aveu à vous faire... je suis nègre. 2654
My dear little godmother I must tell you something... I am a nigger.
Долженъ Вамъ признаться что... я негръ.

Fig. 4-25

Fig. 4-24 is titled Marraines et Poilus (*Godmothers and Soldiers*). *Poilu was the common designation for the French soldier in WWI. The black soldier towers over the French woman, who seems taken aback by his size. We can surmise she had no idea the man she had been writing to was a black African. Large as the African is, he seems very much the "Grand Enfant," and his outreached hands being interpreted as a threat by the young woman more likely express: "Hold on— don't be scared!"*

Also in cartoon format, Fig. 4-25, dated 1919, shows a marraine who is just learning the soldier with whom she has been corresponding is an African. As if his appearance in not proof enough, the Senegalese infantryman tells of the obvious in a confession ("My dear little godmother. I must tell you something. I am a nigger."). Distress at the revelation seems to be felt on both sides. This card's caption is in three languages— French, English, and Russian, the languages of the three major Allies at the start of the war. The French and Russian terms for black person are the standard nègre/negr. The English translation opts for "nigger," a term as derogatory in the early decades of the twentieth century as it is today. Instances were recorded of marraines not knowing their correspondents were Africans, and interestingly enough—at least in fiction of the time—even instances of marraines turning out to be men disguising their gender to the soldiers.[3]

2801

OH! SHOCKING!

Fig. 4-26

Fig. 4-26 depicts a tirailleur wooing a French blonde curled up on an armchair. Both are shown as childlike figures, while hovering above them is a full-sized adult woman who has discovered them and exclaims in English, "Oh! Shocking!" One wonders about the sole use of English on this French card. Is it perhaps because the older woman is an English maid that she is so taken aback? French cards of interracial couplings were surely more likely to render uncomfortable English viewers of the time than their French counterparts. In any case, the situation is treated here with good humor.

Fig.4-27

Fig. 4-28

Figs. 4-27 and 4-28 are the front and back sides of a postcard reserved for military correspondence. On the front are pencil sketches of six tirailleurs sénégalais, each carefully drawn to capture their facial features either in profile or full face frontal. These are welcome departures from the stereotypical portrayals of the African soldiers as large-lipped, smiling, and childlike. The soldier in the center right, though a large-sized figure, seems to be hunched over and a bit defeated looking. To his right is a soldier with tribal scars; to his left, two tirailleurs with earrings. There are no smiles shown here, rather the hardened faces of a tired looking group of fighting men. On the verso are written the names of the six soldiers. At a time when African soldiers were rarely individualized, this simple card drawn by a fellow soldier is a lasting tribute to real men in wartime.

CHAPTER 5

SEMISAVAGE

The transformation in image of the tirailleur from savage to fierce and loyal fighter/grand enfant was not without its contradictions. Once the French realized the terror the tirailleurs sénégalais evoked in the German enemy, they were prone to exploit the "savage" image of their African troops to their advantage. This meant the tirailleur was now both the proud product of the French mission to civilize the African (*mission civilisatrice*) and a savage easily associated with such cruelties as decapitation and cannibalism. Allegations of brutal behavior not in accordance with international law were indeed leveled against the colonial soldiers—especially by the Germans—and many articles in the French press at least initially echoed these charges. Cutting off fingers and ears as trophies, beheadings, massacring prisoners, and cold-blooded use of the coute-coute (machete) in close combat numbered among the most frequent accusations. In the end, there was little evidence that African soldiers behaved any more cruelly than their white counterparts, and apart from the many propagandistic images in illustrations no photo postcards depict mutilations or beheadings.[1] More important was the perception among France's enemies that the black African soldier acted with a savagery out of place among "civilized" nations and France's willingness to exploit that image.

Fig. 5-01

Fig. 5-02

Early in the war the French recognized the terrifying effect the use of black African troops had on their enemies. The caption of a postcard (Fig. 5-01) showing a group of tirailleurs sénégalais in Toulouse dated October 1914 reads in part: "The 1914 War in Toulouse: Our Black Troops – The Senegalese – the Black Terror to the Boche – during their stop in Toulouse." The soldiers stand tall and proud, but are not particularly terrifying in appearance. Their large size, skin color, and tribal scars alone will presumably strike fear in their opponents. More graphic is a card (Fig. 5-02) titled "The War – In Their Culottes." Facing a group of retreating German soldiers, a major is shown holding his nose and asking a young Alsatian boy: "What is that stink?" The boy answers: "It's them, Major, when they saw the Turcos of France, they... shit in their culottes."

SÉRIE HUMORISTIQUE DE LA GUERRE 1914

15 Représailles
— Toâ touyé blessés ?... Moâ corriger toâ... Hi hi hi,
Bono !! Bono !! oreilles de cochon.

Fig. 5-03

— Alors vous ne goupez pas les oreilles aux brisonniers ?
— Non, mon vieux boche... On se contente de leur couper..
leur retraite.   6. - L. E. - Déposé.

Fig. 5-04

Cutting off body parts has never been a particularly rare practice in wartime. One is reminded of the American troops in Vietnam sporting necklaces of cut off Viet Cong ears. In WWI, such accusations were launched by all sides. The "Rape of Belgium" is a classic case in which German soldiers were reported to have cut off the ears and noses of civilians. Because Africans were often regarded by Europeans as savages or near savages by nature, it is not surprising that many of the images of mutilations were ascribed to them. When the Germans protested against alleged savage practices by African troops, the French denied such charges, while at the same time reinforcing such images as part of their propaganda campaign.

In Fig. 5-03, a tirailleur with his machete holds up an ear he has just cut from the head of a German. Part of a "Humor Series of the 1914 War," its caption reads "Reprisals," then in petit nègre the French soldier cries out: "You've been wounded? I'll fix that --- ha ha ha. Good – the ears of a pig." This is the Germans' worst nightmare: to come up against an African soldier, given his reputation for mutilating his enemies. For the joyous tirailleur, the German is likened to a pig, a despised and forbidden symbol in Islam that was the faith of many of the black soldiers.

Far worse is indicated on Fig. 5-04, where a captured German soldier turns to his dark-skinned captor and asks in accented French: "Do you really cut off the ears of prisoners?" The French soldier replies, "No, my dear Boche. We're happy in cutting off"—followed by a pause—"their retreat." The quick pause is just enough to raise the specter of genital mutilation, a concept reinforced by the three undeniably phallic shapes lying in the foreground.

Feminizing the enemy is another standard practice in wartime propaganda, and illustrations hinting at sodomy are not uncommon. In Fig. 5-05, German troops are being overwhelmed in their trenches by the tirailleurs. The caption reads: "Here come the Turcos. Guard Your Asses!!!" The warning need not be limited to a metaphoric interpretation. The perceived threat of sodomy by African black soldiers was widespread among the Germans. Witnesses tell of terrified Germans fearing such, surrendering to the tirailleurs, waving Red Cross flags, and scurrying to climb up over the tops of the trenches with hands at all times raised.[2]

Postcard 5-06, which shows a German soldier being bayonetted in his derriere by an African tirailleur, is worthy of a bit more attention. The French caption above the illustration reads "War 1914," and the one below reads "Sheaths for French bayonets patented by Moltke." Lt. Gen. Kuno Augustus Friedrich Karl Detlev Graf von Moltke (1847–1923) was a military commander and adjutant to Kaiser Wilhelm II. In 1907, he became involved in a scandal in which close members of the Kaiser's entourage were said to be engaging in homosexual acts and threatening the security of the state by being vulnerable to blackmail. The affair, which lasted through 1909, was heavily publicized and was the equivalent in Germany of the Oscar Wilde affair in England. Homosexuality was for the first time openly discussed as charges and counter-charges of libel, blackmail, and depravity emerged. Reputations were ruined, high ranking officials were forced to resign, and prison sentences were handed out. One lasting effect of this scandal was the association of homosexuality with Germans in the coming years, especially by the French and English. Homosexuals seeking liaisons in public toilets in France, for example, would often ask as code, "Parlez-vous allemand?" (Do you speak German?) This explains the reference to Moltke by the postcard's illustrator, and is one of the earliest and relatively rare allusions to homosexuality in the early postcard era. The use of African troops to perform symbolic acts of sodomy by penetrating the enemy was far more common than use of non-African French troops—a phenomenon with racial/sexual implications that could be further explored.[3]

Fig. 5-05

Fig. 5-06

Jef

LE BON BOULOT

Fig. 5-07

Today, beheadings are generally regarded as barbaric, but that has not always been the case. Particularly in the colonization of Africa, indigenous fighters and rebel leaders were often beheaded to serve as warnings to others. In France, beheadings via the guillotine lasted until 1971. In WWI, unsubstantiated reports told of the French military having to put a halt to its African soldiers returning from battle with the heads of enemy soldiers.[4] Upon arriving on French shores, one contingent of tirailleurs sénégalais was met with French crowds shouting, "Bravo riflemen! Cut off the heads of the Germans."[5] In this context, the watercolor image in Fig. 5-07 of a colonial soldier holding the severed heads of Kaiser Wilhelm and Emperor Franz Joseph with the caption "Good Work" would not be surprising. Its purpose was to reinforce the important role African soldiers were said to be playing on the Allies' behalf. On card 5-08, a tirailleur shows off his plunder to a white French soldier with the comment in petit nègre, "These are a few souvenirs for Madame Soudan." They consist of military equipment, shells, uniforms, sausages, and a human skull.

Fig. 5-08

—Ça pitits souvenis pou Madame Soudan

d'É TOUJOU LE CASQUE À LI

Fig. 5-09

The contradiction the French faced wanting to present its African soldiers as savages in battle yet childlike in character is well expressed in Fig. 5-09. A smiling and congenial looking tirailleur stands facing the viewer. In his shoulder bag is a spiked German helmet captured in battle. Closer examination shows the helmet is still atop the severed head of the murdered enemy soldier. It is a chilling revelation.

Le Siège de Paris

Tiens, Petit Trottin, ti rapporté casque à pointe, et sais y a tête dedans.

Fig. 5-10

On a black and white card labeled "The Siege of Paris" (Fig. 5-10), a tirailleur points out to two French women the spiked German helmet he has brought back from battle—with the enemy soldier's head still inside it. The two women express shock, while in the background a third woman looks at herself in the mirror with her new souvenir helmet atop her head. The caption below, in petit nègre, reads: "Look, girls, I've brought you back a [German] spiked helmet and, you see, it still has the head inside it." Sporting the helmet of a murdered soldier may be all the fashion, but to behead him in the process? Now, that is barbaric!

Perhaps the ultimate reflection of savagery for the European was cannibalism. It was a practice associated with diverse cultures, from the South Pacific to wide swaths of Africa. Postcards disseminated by Christian missions in Africa would at times use the term "cannibal" while depicting indigenous people before their conversion. At carnivals and fairs, so-called cannibals would be put on display to pique the fascination of onlookers. As war propaganda, soldiers might be seen metaphorically celebrating victory over the enemy by consuming them, while conjuring up a cannibal nature for the African soldier was a ploy used by the French and Germans for their own purposes.

Fig. 5-11

On a hand painted watercolor signed by artist A. C. dated
October 1, 1914 (Fig. 5-11), a tirailleur sénégalais hands the
severed head of Kaiser Wilhelm over to his child. He exclaims in
petit nègre: "Don't eat him, he's poisoned." The French dilemma
in depicting the African soldier is again apparent. On the one
hand, he is the brave soldier assimilated into the French army
and fighting for his mother country, as witnessed by the captured
German helmet he carries. On the other hand, he is still the savage,
cutting off heads and even offering one to his cannibal son,
notwithstanding the admonition not to eat it because it is poisoned.

Postcard 5-12 pictures an African panorama at the Paris
Universal Exposition in 1900 and is captioned: "N'Asakaras
Women, Preparing their meal." Three women and a child are
shown outside their African village disemboweling a captured
man with feet still bound and preparing the fire to cook him. The
severed head of the victim sits on the ground in front of the child,
while a woman at the back holds his dismembered hand. The
panorama is sponsored by the recent Marchand Mission, a French
expedition (1897–98) into central Africa to counter British expansion
on the continent. Images such as this reinforced in the European
imagination the association of cannibalism with Africans. This
particular exhibition counted over fifty million visitors.[6]

Fig. 5-12

Y a bon ! c'est le boche qui régale !

108. PARIS.

Fig. 5-13

Fig. 5-14

The tirailleur on postcard 5-13 is cooking up his meal using a captured German helmet as a pot.

The caption in petit nègre "It's Good! The Boche is treating me to a good meal!" hints the German soldier may indeed be the main course. In Fig. 5-14, titled "German caricatures: Our Tirailleurs," a black African soldier with exaggeratedly large lips approaches a barrel labeled "sausages and sauerkraut" being held by a German soldier, who says in broken French, "I am lost! A Cannibal!" In the background a tirailleur bayonets an enemy soldier in the rear end.

CARICATURES ALLEMANDES : Nos Tirailleurs

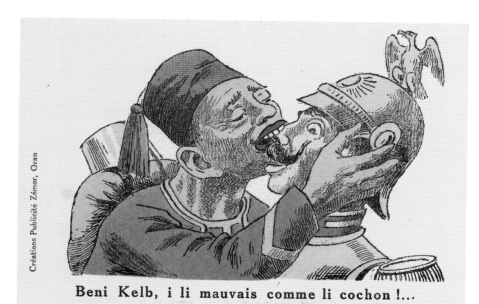

Créations Publicité Zénor, Oran

Beni Kelb, i li mauvais comme li cochon !...

Fig. 5-15

A French card (Fig. 5-15) printed in French Algeria shows an African soldier taking a bite of a German officer. He exclaims: "Sons of Dogs, he tastes bad like a pig!" The cannibalistic act is not up for question, but rather, the bad tasting German whose flavor is compared to that of prohibited pig meat.

Fig. 5-16

A humorous twist on the idea of cannibalism is shown on Fig. 5-16, a black and white hand-drawn postcard. A tirailleur sénégalais in petit nègre comforts two captured German soldiers: "Don't be afraid... my marabout [Muslim religious teacher] prohibits me from eating pig...." The irony is that a faithful Muslim would unquestioningly cannibalize another human being if he were not deemed a pig.

— Qui is qui çi Missé Prusco, à la broche ou tout cru qui ti veux qui ji bouffe ta viande ?
— Massa Prussian ! D'ye want me to eat your flesh roasted or raw ?

Fig. 5-17

In a battle scene (Fig. 5-17) in which wild-eyed African troops are overcoming the Germans with fists, bayonets, and rifle butts, cannibalism is clearly implied when a black soldier asks a German: "Massa Prussian! Do ye want me to eat your flesh roasted or raw?" Interestingly, the action is taking place under the command of a white French officer in the background. The card is bilingual (French and English).

Au Bivouac

A quelle sauce veux-tu qu'on te mange, Guillaume ?

Fig. 5-18

An illustrated French card titled "At Camp" (Fig. 5-18) shows four soldiers representing the Allies roasting alive a naked and chained Kaiser Wilhelm. The three to the left—identifiably Belgian, Russian, and English—tend to him as the French soldier, here depicted as a tirailleur sénégalais, stands ready with an enormous fork. The African is differentiated in having a wild and frenzied look on his face. The caption at the bottom reads: "And what sauce would you like to be eaten with, Wilhelm?"

La Cuisine des Tirailleurs ~ The Skirmishers' Kitchen.
~ti sais Missié Guillaume, ci pas pour nous qu'on ti fait cuire ; ci pour ti soldats qui crivent de faim !....
~ You know Herr Wilhelm, it is not for us that we are roasting you it is for your soldiers who are rather too hungry! ~

Fig. 5-19

An added twist of humor character-izes the image of African cannibalism on card 5-19. Six tirailleurs are roasting alive a naked Kaiser Wilhelm, readying themselves with a fork, knife, and pan. The bilingual (French and English) cap-tion below reads: "The Skirmishers' Kitchen: You know, Herr Wilhelm, it is not for us that we are roasting you – it is for your soldiers who are rather too hungry!"

Fig. 5-20

Fig. 5-21

Consuming the enemy as an article of food is not restricted to images of African cannibalism. In Fig. 5-20, a German postcard presents the weekly menu of a soldier in 1914. Ingredients include enemy fighters from Russia, England, East Austria, Serbia, Montenegro, and Japan. For Monday, Russian eggs with Cossack meat is followed by Tuesday's English beefsteak with bomb supplements. Most dramatically portrayed are Friday's Montenegrin mutton fry freshly stolen—illustrated by a heavyset Montenegrin soldier lying face down on the steaming plate with three knives in his back—and Saturday's menu of skewered Japanese bird of prey, showing a caged Japanese-headed bird about to be skewered by a German soldier.

A formal menu is presented on postcard 5-21, headed by notice of a last-minute menu change due to Germany's having been turned back from Paris, where the "very heavy" Emperor of the Boches had been planning a victory feast. Parody in the naming of ingredients takes in the Belgians, Cossacks, and Gen. Joffre among others. At the top left, four tirailleurs sénégalais have skewered the naked Kaiser above a fire and stand ready to eat him with a fork and knife.

The choice of African soldiers to represent the capture of Wilhelm followed by their cannibalization of him again calls attention to the French dilemma of needing to portray the African soldier as the product of the French civilizing mission, yet encourage his depiction as a ruthless savage to scare the Germans.

CHAPTER 6

EXOTIC CANNIBAL

The German response to the presence of French African troops on European battlefields was, as for the French, not without its contradictions. Foremost, German propaganda railed against the use of African troops in Europe as an insult to civilized behavior and to Germany itself. It was degrading for a German to have to subject himself to the possibility of fighting, not to mention being killed, by an African savage on European soil.[1] Making matters worse was the plethora of French postcards depicting German soldiers and officers being humiliated at the hands of black troops. On their postcards, the Germans portrayed black African soldiers as fanatical and brutal, and the captured soldiers as broken and defeated men. Still, there are instances where the treatment of the African soldier is more sympathetic. The prime examples are black prisoners displayed as exotic curiosities, and artists' portraits of African prisoners in which individual character is allowed to surface. Also, for purposes of propaganda, some German cards depicted the humane treatment of its Muslim prisoners—many dark-skinned—to encourage colonial troops to desert the Allied cause and join Germany and Turkey in jihad against France and Britain. This contradiction of African as savage and Germany as the friend of Muslims, regardless of skin color, invites an interesting comparison to the French dilemma, where black African forces are presented as proof of the success of France's civilizing mission yet, at the same time, are promoted as savages to frighten the Huns.

Understanding German perspectives on race and racial difference during WWI offers insight into the ways French African prisoners were portrayed on the postcard. Though all the European colonial powers incorporated a biologically based racial hierarchy in their political framework, in Germany, interest and public discussion on the topic was far more developed. As evidence, the German government sponsored two studies of their prisoners of war. The first, the Royal Prussian Phonographic Commission—composed of anthropologists, linguists, and ethnologists—recorded the music and various languages and dialects of its subjects. Between 1915 and 1918, more than seventy prisoner of war camps were visited and recordings were made in over 250 languages.[2] The second study had as its goal the measure of the physical features of prisoners, photographing them, and classifying them into racial hierarchies. Wilhelm Doegen, the leader of the first study, wrote after the war: "Germany did not fight against a world of armies ... but rather against a world of races."[3]

Countless photo postcards, as well as artists' illustrations, focus on the racial diversity of prisoners. As on French cards, "type" is the standard term to designate a "race" or ethnic grouping. On many of the cards, the black African soldiers are positioned in such a way as to highlight their difference in skin color from other captives. Here they appear more like exotic trophies than simply French soldiers, and are regularly identified as "Senegalese" or "Blacks" instead of simply "French."

German postcards depicting imprisoned African soldiers in a more humane manner were used to demonstrate the everyday normality of prison life and counter reports of dismal camp conditions and prisoner abuse. On one such card, a black tirailleur at a prisoner of war camp is shown in a theatrical piece as the object of affection of two cross-dressed soldiers. Artists' sketches also depict individual African prisoners rather sympathetically, even if the subjects are left unnamed. Far more fascinating from a historical perspective are cards related to the prisoner of war camp at Zossen, Germany, popularly known as the *Halbmondlager* (Crescent Moon Camp). The camp was the brainchild of a German aristocrat and diplomat named Max von Oppenheim. It was part of a propaganda campaign calling for jihad that would try to redirect the allegiances of the Muslim prisoners to the cause of the Ottoman Empire and its German ally, while at the same time inciting uprisings among the Muslim populations in Africa and India against their French and English colonial masters. In November 1914, the Sultan, in accord with Germany, declared that Britain, France, and Russia were enemies of Islam, and in November 1915, a camp newspaper called *al-Djihâd* began publication. Muslim prisoners at the camp were given special privileges, such as better-than-average rations and clothing and access to a new mosque (actually the first constructed on German soil) modeled on the Dome of the Rock and rumored to have been personally financed by the Kaiser. Postcards reflect life at the camp, with prisoners playing sports, engaging in the preparation of halal meats, and emerging from prayer. In spite of the heavy-handed politics at work, the campaign did generate highly positive images of the dark-skinned prisoners at a time when such images by Germans were rare.

"Ihr, die ihr Triebe
Des Herzens kennt,
Sprecht: ist es Liebe,
Was hier so brennt?"

Entente cordiale.

Fig. 6-01

A rather curious postcard sent by German military mail (feldpost) in 1917 (Fig. 6-01) pictures Marianne—the symbol for France—asking a black soldier whether or not it is really love that is burning in her heart. Marianne, a rather gaunt and unattractive figure, has her hand on her heart as she faces the equally made-to-look-unattractive African soldier with his bumpy features. The card's title, Entente cordiale (Cordial Agreement), alludes to the name given to a series of military agreements beginning in 1904 between France and Britain. A likely purpose of the card is to denigrate the French for their close relationship with the Africans they were recruiting for military service on European soil.

Early in the war, French propaganda began to feature postcards showing German soldiers, especially officers, being captured and humiliated by African fighters. This was projected as the ultimate indignity that could happen to a German, given his propensity of regarding black troops as savages. An entire subset of French postcards reflect this German image of the African put into a position—thanks to France—of being able to disgrace the German combatant. On postcard 6-02, a tirailleur with sword drawn slams his metal cooking pot on the head of a captured German as its contents pour down over his face. The caption above reads: "Humorous Series of the 1914 War," while below, under the title "A Good Vengeance by a Turco" we find, in petit nègre: "You will respect me,,,the prisoner doesn't want to follow the orders of an officer! You'll carry my bag – and then – my mess and kit!"

Fig. 6-03 has a more involved narrative, purportedly taken from a French newspaper. Here, the story details a Turco's good fortune capturing a German officer. After disarming him he begins to lead the captive away, but the angry German turns around and injures him. At first the Turco thinks of beating him, but decides on a better tactic. He will humiliate the German officer by forcing him to carry his bag and all his gear under threat of his bayonet. In this way the colonial soldier returns triumphantly to camp with his captive.

SÉRIE HUMORISTIQUE DE LA GUERRE 1914

Une Bonne Revanche d'un Turco

Toã rouspéter .. prisonnier pas vouloir suivre... officier ! faire le malin... toã porter sac... et puis... toã coiffer gamelle !
XVI

Fig. 6-02

Fig. 6-03

A pun and racial slur can be found on another card (6-04) depicting the humiliation of a German by a black soldier. An African chases a German soldier, pricking him in his behind with his bayonet. The text reads: "The Bicot: You are afraid of my black mug? No need to be, my weapon is white." Bicot is a French ethnic slur usually applied to Arabs, while the term for bladed weapon in French is arme blanche (white weapon). The card manages to demean the German and the black tirailleur.

Fig. 6-04

Fig. 6-05

Other means of symbolically humiliating the enemy include caging him and putting him on public display as one would a wild beast. Fig. 6-05 does just that, with an imprisoned Kaiser guarded over by an armed African soldier. The caption reads: "The stirring capture of a beast of prey of the Hun race, family of Hohenzollern, of bloodthirsty instinct, carried out at the imperial palace of Berlin. This beast only knows burglary, felonies, etc." It is an interesting turn of fortune, as Africans were often put on public display by the French and the Germans at world fairs to the curiosity of onlookers. Here the African guard is barefoot, implying he is not all that removed from his primitive roots.

In Fig. 6-06, a German soldier is being ridden by an African soldier with a whip and prodded on by another sticking a bayonet into his rear. The caption reads: "Keep on marching or you die, dirty pig!" The German is no better than an animal.

A card of similar manufacture (Fig. 6-07) pictures an African soldier aiming a miniature cannon at two of his German enemies. The men stand by a trench with empty liquor bottles strewn about. The African forces the Germans to dance with one another, remarking: "Ah! You're drinking good liquor, you idiots! Dance now – Here's the music."

Ti marches ou ti crèves, sale Cochon !...

Fig. 6-06

Ah! ti bois li bon liqueur, bougr' di Cochons !...

Danse, maint'nant voilà la mousique

Fig. 6-07

Drunkenness on the part of the German enemy resurfaces in Fig. 6-08, where a group of tirailleurs sénégalais have come upon three besotted soldiers. One German has passed out amidst the overturned bottle and glasses. The card's caption is "The Turcos!," while below, the African soldiers cry out "Prussians! Good, Good," using the Y a bon phrase invariably associated with the black tirailleurs.

A far more complex image of German humiliation is depicted in Fig. 6-09. Two German soldiers cuddle with one another on a sofa-like structure in an effeminate manner meant to evoke illicit intimacy while a third looks on, perhaps enviously. An African tirailleur, manly looking and with bulging arm muscles, offers them a tray of apples and bananas arranged to simulate male genitals. On the table is a bottle of water from the River Meuse, recalling the German defeat during the Meuse-Argonne Offensive in 1918. Below is the caption "German morals," reinforcing the message that Germans are perverse in their tastes; above, the tirailleur says: "Here are some large ones and some beautiful ones. If you have the desire, guys." The African soldier, no longer in the role of the grand enfant, has become a sexualized being, offering illicit phallic delights and symbolically even himself for the pleasure of the homosexualized German enemy.

Fig. 6-08

Fig. 6-09

On postcard 6-10, Germans exact revenge for French propaganda showing their soldiers being humiliated by black Africans. A German soldier is pictured grabbing a tirailleur sénégalais by the ear and proclaiming: "Captain, I'm bringing you a Turco, excuse me if he's not the most handsome!" Indeed, the illustrator has made a special effort to portray the black soldier in as negative a light as possible. His entire face seems covered in hair and his mouth drawn exaggeratedly large. Pulling the Turco by his ear echoes the stereotype of the African cutting off the enemy's ears for souvenirs or good luck charms. The verso (Fig. 6-11) shows the card to be a feldkarte (field card) designed for free use by the military. Printed at the top of the back side are spaces for the sender's name and his division, regiment, and company. The card is no doubt meant to dispel the myth of the formidable, brute savage that was said to be frightening so many German soldiers.

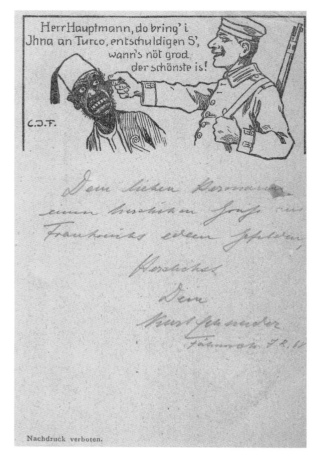

Fig. 6-10

Fig. 6-11

Fig. 6-12

In Fig. 6-12, a Hussar officer is leading the cavalry forward, his white steed jumping over a fallen tirailleur sénégalais. Ground troops move forward in the background. The caption for this artfully drawn and highly patriotic illustration is "Let's Get em!" The African soldier has been singled out as the target; does he serve only as a symbol for France, or is there a particular satisfaction for the German viewer in seeing the humiliation and defeat of one of the "savages" deployed against them on the battlefield by the French?

A devastating attack against French African forces is pictured in Fig. 6-13, where the Senegalese, we are told in a caption on the back, have charged the German trenches in a nighttime offensive.

The black soldiers, carrying knives and rifles, are no match for the German machine guns. It is a resounding defeat for the Africans, portrayed here as especially vulnerable and incompetent. A town burns on a hill in the background.

Fig. 6-13

Gott strafe England!

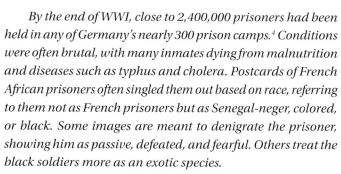

Auf dem französischen Kriegsschauplatz gefangener Kannibale (Menschenfresser)
ein Kämpfer „für Kultur."

Fig. 6-14

I COLLABORATORI DELL'INGHILTERRA.

Fig. 6-15

By the end of WWI, close to 2,400,000 prisoners had been held in any of Germany's nearly 300 prison camps.[4] Conditions were often brutal, with many inmates dying from malnutrition and diseases such as typhus and cholera. Postcards of French African prisoners often singled them out based on race, referring to them not as French prisoners but as Senegal-neger, colored, or black. Some images are meant to denigrate the prisoner, showing him as passive, defeated, and fearful. Others treat the black soldiers more as an exotic species.

Fig. 6-14 depicts a captured French African soldier barechested and looking somewhat stunned. At the top of the card is "God Punish England," a phrase commonly found on many German propaganda cards, while below "From the French War Front a captured cannibal [Man- eater], a fighter for 'Culture.'" Cannibalism, as mentioned in chapter 5, was the

iconic symbol of savagery for Europeans, and the irony from the German perspective of the French employing a man-eater to preserve "culture" is not lost.

Italy was initially an ally of the Central Powers, but remained out of WWI until 1915, when it decided to join the side of the Allies. Fig. 6-15, an Italian card, pictures England's collaborators in the war. Although it derisively satirizes the Scots and colonial Indian forces, it is the image of the African that stands out—large lipped, ape-like, naked except for a skirt-like garment, and holding a bottle of brandy. The Indian soldier may have just beheaded an enemy soldier with his knife, but it is the African who truly represents savagery. The association of the black colonial fighting forces with an inherent African primitiveness persists, regardless whether or not they are defending their French or British motherland.

Fig. 6-16

Germans viewed the large mix of races and ethnic groupings they held in prisoner of war camps with a fascination and an understanding that the captured soldiers represented inferior cultures. In Fig. 6-16, a home guard stands watch over a group of prisoners ranging from Scots and black Africans to Indians. He acknowledges their wide range of racial and ethnic backgrounds (white, black, yellow, brown, races of people from all the world). The guard then observes the prisoners arguing back and forth as to who is the true guardian of European culture. Though these "freedom fighters" regard the Germans as "barbarians," the guard watching over these Zouaves, Indians, and Russians looks at these "fighters for culture" and laughs. There is no doubt in his mind that the motley crew behind the fence, despite their delusions, are the real barbarians. The card was sent as feldpost in June 1916.

Senegal-Neger, welche auf französischer Seite gegen unsere Truppen kämpfen, als Kriegsgefangene in Darmstadt.

Fig. 6-17

The grouping of French African prisoners for display is a common feature on WWI German postcards. In Fig. 6-17, three of the five have visible wounds as they line up in front of their captors. Facial expressions range from sadness to resentment. The caption above reads "War Year 1914/15," while below the photograph: "Senegal Negroes [Neger], who fought on the French side against our troops, as war prisoners in Darmstadt." The German word *neger* was arguably not used at the time pejoratively, though opinions vary.[5]

The soldiers captured in Fig. 6-18 are identified as *Senegalschützen* ("Senegalese Shooters")—a more respectful term—though the caption refers to them as France's "Big ones," recalling the phrase, "How the Mighty Have Fallen."

Fig. 6-18

Farbige französische Gefangene beim Wasserholen

Fig. 6-19

On postcard image 6-19, the black soldiers are referred to as "colored" ("Colored French prisoners at the water hole.") They stand, water pails in hand, in front of an armed guard at the steps of a building. In Fig. 6-20, the black soldiers are not separated for display. However, here too they are uniquely identified by color. The caption to the right reads: "Our prisoners on the Western Front," while below is written: "Englishmen, Scots, French, Alpine Fighters, Zuaves, Blacks (Schwarze)."

Unsere Gegner an der Westfront

Engländer, Schotten, Franzosen, Alpenjäger, Zuaven, Schwarze

Fig. 6-20

Jumbo
bei Douaumont gefangen genommen

409

Fig. 6-21

"Jumbo" is the name given to the black French soldier on Fig. 6-21. Though large in stature, he is shown in defeat and fearful looking. The caption tells he was taken prisoner in Douaumont, a village in northeastern France that was totally destroyed in the war with over 100,000 French and German fatalities.

CHAPTER 6

Fig. 6-22

Fig. 6-23

A postcard labeled "Prisoners of War" (Fig. 6-22) lines up six captives and identifies them by nation of origin or ethnicity: Scot, Belgian, French, Turco, Zouave, and English. In the German prisoner of war camps over thirteen nationalities were documented, representing scores of ethnicities.

A colored card from Kleinwittenberg Camp (Fig. 6-23) displays in oval frames above the camp five prisoners varying in origin from black African to Indian. The African is top center, giving him a certain prominence over the others.

Fig. 6-24 is a cartoon card highlighting the varied backgrounds of Germany's captured soldiers. A German guard sits watch on a French train marked "To Berlin" as three prisoners poke their heads out the window: a French soldier, a tirailleur sénégalais, and a Scot smoking a pipe. The translated caption reads: "On the Way to Berlin."

Auf dem Wege nach Berlin

Fig. 6-24

LA COSECHA EN ALEMANIA : VERANO DE 1915

Fig. 6-25

The German fascination with the ethnic and racial variety of its enemy forces is reflected on an illustrated card (Fig. 6-25) from Spain, a country that remained neutral throughout the war. Prisoners of every type, including Scottish, French, and Russian, work under guard collecting the harvest. Among them are several tirailleurs sénégalais, the most prominent kneeling bottom center. The card is titled "The Harvest in Germany: Summer 1915." Of the 1,450,000 prisoners the Germans captured, approximately 750,000 were put to work in agriculture, helping to replace able-bodied men sent to war.[6]

Wünsdorf-Zossen   Moschee

Mohammedaner

Fig. 6-26

Fig. 6-26 served as part of the German propaganda campaign to entice Muslim soldiers fighting for England and France to join forces with Germany and Muslim Turkey to wage jihad against the Allies. Images of the ornate mosque at Zossen and the array of Muslim prisoners were meant to project a positive image and dispel any notions of prejudice on the part of Germans toward Muslims generally.

Similarly, Fig. 6-27 shows a group of Muslim male prisoners in varied dress emerging from the mosque in Zossen. It reads: "From one of our Moslem prisoner of war camps - Leaving the Mosque."

Aus einem unserer mohammedanischen Gefangenenlager   Beim Verlassen der Moschee

Fig. 6-27

Fig. 6-28

In Fig. 6-28—a 1916 photo card from the German prisoner of war camp in Cottbus, Germany—a tirailleur sénégalais is being wooed by two white European soldiers in full drag. Cottbus and an adjacent camp nearby boasted British, French, and Russian theaters. Theatrical productions were common in the camps and provided a welcome distraction for the internees. Meanwhile, cards such as these projected an image of prisoner well-being and were useful as German propaganda.

Fig. 6-29

Fig. 6-30

Fig. 6-29 is a sympathetic portrait of a black prisoner of war titled "A Turco (Negro from the Sudan)." It is artistically executed by signed artist E. Günkol, and shows a relaxed figure smoking his pipe. On the verso is stamped "War Commemorative Card." The card has been mailed as feldpost.

Another portrait card (Fig. 6-30) is titled "Black Frenchman (Senegal-Negro)" and signed Max Rabes, one of Germany's best known artists before the war. Rabes painted Orientalist subjects, as well as works depicting various aspects of WWI. A black and white illustration titled "Russian POWs from 1916" is one of his most memorable. Here, a black French soldier is shown with dignity and compassion.

CHAPTER 7
LEGACIES

The legacy of France's black African soldiers in WWI is multifaceted. The French, Germans, and Africans all played a role in how the soldiers are remembered or not remembered. As remarkable as the large body of research and discussion on WWI emanating from Europe is, there is, nonetheless, a marked paucity of material reflecting the experiences and views of the tirailleurs.[1] Postcards mostly reflect the manipulations of black soldiers' images by the individual European countries to promote their own narratives and myths regarding the war, so many aspects of war's reality have been distorted or left undepicted.

For the French, the remaking of the image of the African from savage to well-disciplined fighter resulted in an outpouring of praise lauding his accomplishments and their origins in the mission civilisatrice. As WWI progressed, and long after its finish, emphasis was placed increasingly on the African soldier not only as an able conscript, but as an assimilated member of the French nation, a black Frenchman willing to give his life for his mother country and its ideals of *liberté*, *égalité*, and *fraternité*. French metropolitan and colonial soldiers, blacks, whites, Asians, and Arabs were all seen as having united with common interests in a common struggle during the war. Monuments commemorating the sacrifices of colonial troops in particular were erected in France and abroad, victory parades were organized, and honors were given. Altruism was only part of the picture. France needed to counter the ongoing German charges it had used bloodthirsty

cannibals on the European battleground and was undeserving of the victory it later claimed.

German complaints about the use of blacks on European soil turned especially vitriolic immediately after the war, when the Versailles Treaty allowed for a fifteen-year occupation of the German Rhineland. Approximately 40,000 of the soldiers assigned were to come from France's African colonial empire, and 5,000 black African troops served in 1919 and 1920.[2] The popular press in Germany, which referred to all dark-skinned soldiers as inherently inferior, called their deployment *Die Schwatze Schmach* (The Black Shame). African troops were deliberately placed in the Rhineland, according to its argument, to further humiliate the Germans in their defeat. Their deployment was both a crime against humanity and a betrayal of the white race. The German press talked of savagery and mass rape, even though studies conducted in the aftermath of the war had already shown many of the German accusations to be unsubstantiated (instances of war crimes were no more prevalent among the colonial troops than among the white soldiers). The children resulting from relations between the black soldiers and German women were commonly referred to as "Rhineland bastards." Sterilization of the children was advocated by the right wing and later, under the Nazis, approximately 385 were indeed sterilized.[3] France eventually relented in the deployment of black troops in the Rhineland, due in part to pressure from the United States and Britain.

The vicious stereotypes regarding blacks persisted. In Hitler's *Mein Kampf* in 1925, the future Führer refers to the presence of black troops in France as leading to the pollution and negrification of their race. Italian posters in WWII showed America's black soldiers wantonly ransacking Christian churches, and the Vatican at one point requested that Allied forces ban black soldiers from occupying liberated Rome for fear of mass rape.[4] One consequence of this campaign of bigotry and hate was the deliberate massacre in 1940 of thousands of tirailleur sénégalais prisoners by the Germans in their conquest of France.

Given that most war-related postcards served as propaganda during WWI and reflected the official views of the great powers, it is not surprising many of the harsher realities regarding the deployment of the tirailleurs remained undocumented on this medium. Campaigns before and during the early years of the war to recruit West Africans, for example, often met with active and passive resistance. Thousands of Africans fled into the bush or emigrated to British West Africa to avoid being conscripted. Others maimed themselves or committed suicide, and some took to arms.[5] The quota systems for recruitment placed upon village chiefs often led to kidnapping of families as a means of enticing the runaways to return. French colonial officials generally looked the other way in spite of the obvious comparisons their recruitment policies had to practices under slavery. Postcards depicting the recruitment and training of the Senegalese fighters show only an orderly process being undertaken. Meanwhile, charges that Africa's black soldiers, at least initially, were deliberately placed in the front lines to lead "suicidal" attacks or as shock troops to scare the enemy was a matter open to discussion at the time, but not the subject of postcards.

In spite of the intense campaign to project the Senegalese fighter as patriotically dedicated to defending French values, the truth is large numbers of black African soldiers were unwilling conscripts who had little understanding of European politics. Joe Lunn, in *Memoirs of the Maelstrom: A Senegalese Oral History of the First World War*, quotes one tirailleur:

The men who took us to France to fight knew the reasons they were fighting, but we only knew that we had to fight for them. That was the only thing I knew. Personally I was never told reasons [for the war]. More commonly, the soldiers were told simply that the Boches were bad people and that they despised Blacks.[6]

By WWII, French methods of indoctrination were far more refined and attention was given to assure the African recruits knew why they were fighting and how it supposedly served their interests.

On a more positive note, the opportunities provided by the war for West Africans and the French to interface personally led to a broader understanding and tolerance on both sides. Joe Lunn traces this important development through eyewitness accounts of war veterans. For the French especially, the African was now more a human being than the threatening savage they had once thought him to be. Indeed, in the aftermath of the war, *Négrophilie* played an integral role in the development of French modernism. Black Africans and black culture were now seen as the key to the restoration of the European soul so blinded by its overreliance on rationality.

Black music, style, and dance became all the rage. Though still rooted in racism, albeit a less pernicious form, this attraction of French white society to the "primitive" black African in harmony with nature generated a greater tolerance and influenced artists and intellectuals for decades to come.

The Africans' experience of war in Europe also had a large impact on colonial society when the soldiers returned to their towns and villages. The relative freedoms and fair treatment they experienced abroad rendered it all the more difficult to return to a colonial system hardly changed. Having now fought and given their lives for the mother country, the veterans and their supporters intensified their campaigns to achieve French citizenship for all Senegalese. Importantly, the West Africans' experience of the war in Europe exposed them to new ways of thinking and viewing themselves, and the consequent understandings and confidence it instilled in many of the fighters set off a dynamic that later led to the growth of African independence movements.

With time, later generations in Africa would more likely ascribe to the view that the tirailleurs had been used merely as pawns, if not cannon fodder, by the French in consolidating their African holdings and fighting their European and Asian wars. The very icon of black African service to the French, the Grand Enfant as embodied by the figure on the Banania ads (see Fig. 4-01), would later come under attack when Léopold Senghor—author, statesman, and the first president of independent Senegal—wrote in 1948, in one of his verses: *je déchirerai les rires banania sur tous les murs de France* ("I will tear off the banania grins from all the walls of France").[7]

The modern world had never before seen such wanton destruction on so large a scope as it did during WWI. The dead alone numbered ten million within the military and seven million among civilians. Empires were destroyed and new nations born. The promises of technology and progress in the decades before 1914 turned into a nightmare, as technology had now been applied to devising some of the most hideous horrors one could imagine, including poison gas and widespread aerial bombings of cities. Notwithstanding the charges and countercharges of "barbarism" on the part of the combatting powers, the very nature of civilization and what constitutes civilized behavior was now open to question.

In conclusion, it is worth noting the motivation behind the Europeans' manufacture and manipulation of the images of the French black colonial soldier was not an isolated phenomenon. Instances of the "othering" of a subjugated people by those with the power to exploit them can be found throughout history. An example of this practice closer to home is the change in popular culture of the image of African-Americans from happy child-like slaves singing in the cotton fields to that of threatening aggressors. If before the Civil War Southern society found it opportune to depict slavery as a beneficent institution, after emancipation and the political empowerment of blacks, especially in the South, a different image was needed. Those in power, now seeing their privileges as threatened, proceeded to portray blacks as a social menace, ignorant brutes incapable of responsibly exerting their democratic rights and a threat to white women. Certainly, one of the most important lessons for those seeking freedom is rejecting the images projected on them by their oppressors and taking control over their own self-representation.

« Tous ont voulu combattre pour la défense,
soit de la Mère patrie, soit de la Mère d'adoption. »

Gaston DOUMERGUE, Ministre des Colonies.

Fig. 7-01

Fig. 7-02

A postcard affirming the commonality of interest of all of greater France's subjects in fighting the war is expressed in Fig. 7-01. Marianne stands with flag in hand over six soldiers: three who could be characterized as West African, two North African, and one from France. The caption is a quote from Gaston Doumerge, minister of the colonies and later president of France: "Everyone wanted to fight for her defense, be it for their Mother country or for their Mother [country] by adoption."

On an illustrated French postcard (Fig. 7-02), a white officer questions a towering black tirailleur as to why he is fighting with the French. The other soldiers in the barracks, both black and white, listen in.

"You're not French, you're a Negro, why are you fighting?"
"Madame La France is a good mother, she has children who are white and children who are black, and it is up to all of her children to defend their mother."

There can be no question that France's colonial subjects and the citizens of France, regardless of color, share the same principles and goals that are worth fighting for.

France's black African soldiers participated in all of the major battles of WWI as it unfolded, not only on the Western Front, but also in the Balkans, Mesopotamia, the Middle East, and in Africa. Numerous monuments were raised in their tribute. In the early 1920s, a commission was established that decided on identical monuments: one in Reims, where colonial forces prevented the city from falling to German occupation; and one in Bamako—now in Mali, but formerly the capital of French Sudan. The dedication of the Reims monument took place in 1924. The bronze sculpture atop a pedestal (Fig. 7-03) shows four colonial soldiers, in front of whom stands a white officer holding a French flag. The black soldiers are realistically portrayed, and their facial features indicate more than one ethnic origin. It was one of the most well-known of the monuments to African fighters erected. In 1940, it was dismantled by the Germans, no doubt to be melted into weaponry, and was not replaced until 1963, this time with a modern design.

Another monument dedicated to Gen. Charles Mangin, who first proposed in 1910 the use of black African troops on European soil, suffered a similar fate at the hands of the Germans. In fact, upon Hitler's command, one of the first tasks of the Germans who entered Paris in 1940 was to demolish two specific statues: one of Gen. Mangin, the other of Edith Cavell, the British nurse sentenced to death for treason.[8] Germans had remained incensed at Mangin, first for his role in deploying African troops in the Occupation of the Rhine, and secondly for his response to the Germans after ordering their mayors to provide brothels for the occupying French soldiers. When the mayors refused, complaining about having to establish brothels for Senegalese "gorillas," Gen. Mangin allegedly replied: "German women are none too good for my Senegalese."[9]

The fate of the war monuments, especially those in Africa, presents an interesting story. Some remain intact, others have been dismantled and re-erected in France, while still others, after independence was achieved from the colonial power, were relocated to more remote spaces or removed from public view altogether. The sentiments and even wordings on the tributes ("Allegiance," "Motherland," etc.) reflected a colonial narrative that was no longer welcome in many of the newly independent states.

A. BLUYSEN, Architecte - P. MOREAU-VAUTHIER, Statuaire.

101. - REIMS. — Groupe du Monument aux Héros de l'Armée Noire.

Fig. 7-03

Fig. 7-04

On Bastille Day (July 14, 1919), a victory parade was held in Paris in which Allied forces marched under the Arc de Triomphe and along the Champs-Élysées led by Marshals Joseph Joffre, Ferdinand Foch, and Philippe Pétain. Hundreds of thousands of troops participated. Fig. 7-04 pictures France's Troupes Noires. African-American soldiers were not allowed by the US Army to participate.

A proud black African veteran of WWI displays his medals in Fig. 7-05. He is identified only as *Moktar Sow, vieux serviteur de la France, with no indication of ethnic or geographic origin. The choice of vieux serviteur (former server) over ancien combattant (former combatant) accents his fidelity to a cause—in this case France's military interests—rather than his role as a fighter. Fig. 7-06, showing newly drafted men reporting for duty in Dakar—like card 1-11 showing a recruitment scene—serves to distort a more truthful picture of West African recruitment. In addition to the men who willingly or not entered the French military, there were untold numbers who resisted by fleeing into the bush, with armed resistance, or even self-mutilation.*

5. Moktar Sow, vieux serviteur de la France

Fig. 7-05

2046. Afrique Occidentale
DAKAR — Tirailleurs Sénégalais - Le Rapport

Fig. 7-06

Fig. 7-07

Fig. 7-08

The French at the end of WWI were convinced that only by occupying the German lands west of the Rhine River and safeguarding its many bridges could the world be assured Germany would not rise again and instigate another war. Card 7-07 depicts "The Watch on the Rhine" (La Garde au Rhin or Die Wacht am Rhein) with a North African tirailleur on guard. It was the deployment of non-white troops such as these that Germany so adamantly protested.

In accordance with the Treaty of Versailles in 1919, Germany was forced to take responsibility for the war and pay reparations, mostly to France. The costs to Germany were enormous, and before long it was defaulting on a regular basis. By the beginning of 1923, there had been thirty-four defaults in coal delivery alone.[10] France's Premier Raymond Poincaré decided on January 11 to invade and occupy the Ruhr area east of the Rhine and the center of Germany's coal, iron, and steel production. This led to a campaign of passive resistance by the Germans that failed due largely to the mounting inflation and unemployment plaguing the country. Anger by Germans at their government's capitulation to French demands helped hasten the rise of the far right and fascism in Germany. Fig. 7-08 commemorates the invasion of the Ruhr in 1923, and refers to Poincaré's tarnishing his reputation in the lust for German coal. A black African soldier stands guard with others as the French plunder Germany's coal wealth. Profits from the sale of the card we are told on the verso will go to support the citizens of the Ruhr.

Der eine ist aus Senegal, | Im Rheinland stiehlt der Neger, | Ein jeder sorgt auf seine Weis'
Der andere heißt Dolezal; | Der Tschech' in Prag und Eger: | Für Frankreichs Ehre, Ruhm und Preis.

Fig. 7-09

On card 7-09, two soldiers are being demonized. To the right, a Czech is holding a hand grenade and has his arm around a French African tirailleur. He represents the taking of land from Germany to create the new nation Czechoslovakia. The soldier on the left is identified as a Neger from Senegal. A symbol of savagery for the Germans whose country he helped occupy, the tirailleur holds a bloodied knife between his teeth. It is the coute-coute so much feared by the Germans that according to rumors was used by the African troops to mutilate their enemies. A parody of the French national motto Fraternité, Egalité, Liberté *is draped below: "Brutalité – Bestialité – Egalité!*

During Germany's eight-month passive resistance campaign to protest the invasion of the Ruhr region, many store windows and street kiosks displayed placards in support of raising funds and remaining strong and true to the struggle. In addition, pictures were displayed showing French soldiers beating German civilians. Fig. 7-10 is titled: "The German doesn't forget/Through generations of slave labor." A brutal looking French black soldier slams his rifle butt against a kneeling German farm worker.

Fig. 7-10

An die Deutſchen!

Mahnruf verfaßt für die „Deutſche Tagung"
der Reichsflagge am 20./21. Oktober 1922

von Rudolf Kötter.

* * *

Es raſſeln die Trommeln mit fremdem Klang,
die verruchten Trommeln am deutſchen Rhein,
es brach die Brut mit Siegergeſang,
mit dem frechen, erlog'nen in Straßburg ein:
Vom Münſter web'n die Trikoloren!
Schande, ſind wir für dich geboren?

Es lauert am Rheine das ſchwarze Getier,
das zur Schande die Peſt noch ins Land uns trieb,
es reißt uns vom Munde die teufliſche Gier
das letzte Stück Brot, das uns übrig blieb:
Und glorreich web'n die Trikoloren!
Schande, ſind wir für dich geboren?

Verflucht iſt das Volk, das die Schande nicht ſpürt,
das nicht Tag und nicht Nacht nach der Freiheit lechzt,
das den Willen zur Wehr nicht zum Ziele erkürt,
wenn ſchon gierig der Rabe am Galgen krächzt:
Verflucht iſt das Volk und iſt verloren!
Schande, ſind wir für dich geboren?

So ſchämt Euch der Striemen im deutſchen Geſicht
und küßt nicht dem Feind länger Peitſche und Schuh
und reifet zum rächenden Gottesgericht
und gönnt Euch nicht Frieden noch Freude und Ruh
bis der Racheruf geboren,
bis es brauſt in Herz und Ohren:

„Zerſchlagt ihre Trommeln am deutſchen Rhein,
dieſe Trommeln mit ihrem verruchten Klang
und brecht in die Brut der Bedrücker ein
und erſtickt ſie am eigenen Siegergeſang
Vom Münſter reißt die Trikoloren!
Freiheit, für dich ſind wir geboren!"

* * *

Verlegt bei Fr. Monninger, Nürnberg, Maxplatz 42/44.

Fig. 7-11

Fig. 7-12

A plea to Germans to resist the French occupation of the German Rhineland and seek vengeance is printed on card 7-11. Alluding to the atrocities committed by the French, the reader is repeatedly asked in refrain: "For shame, is it this for which we were born? It is the black beast [das schwarze Getier] which has brought shame [Schande] and the plague [Pest] into our land." The language corresponds closely to the pictorial images of the African occupying forces as beasts, apes, and cannibals. The last line reads: "Freedom, It is for you we were born!"

A postcard printed in March 1924 and sold to raise funds for helping the victims of the occupation (Fig. 7-12) depicts civilian women and children being herded away by African troops—both North African Arab and black Senegalese—under the watch of a French solider in red trousers. The mounted Arab raises a long whip against the civilians. The card is a tribute to those in the Palatinate region (Rheinland-Pfalz) of Germany, and at the top, scenes of devastation by the French in 1674 and 1689 can be seen. Images such as these were powerful propaganda in the postwar period and would lead to dire consequences, especially for black French soldiers in the war to follow.

Fig. 7-13

In contrast to German propaganda cards decrying the occupation of their territory by black beasts, Fig. 7-13—a photo postcard—depicts French Gen. Mangin of the French Army of the Rhine saluting his troops—many of them of African origin—in the occupied city Wiesbaden. The picture is of a well-disciplined army and certainly served French interests in combatting the German stereotypes of African troops running wild and victimizing innocent German civilians. The card is dated April 2, 1921, the same year the Wiesbaden Agreement was signed outlining the reparations the French were to receive from the defeated Germans.

أنجال السنغال بأنواع الحا بهم الونية ينيتة بعسكرهم وطمم جنوب فرنسا

Fig. 7-14

While serving the French, the tirailleurs were often torn between two conflicting identities. On one hand, they were proud members of their native African cultures with many rich traditions; on the other, they were being encouraged to assimilate into a European French culture in many ways quite foreign to them. There can be little doubt that while in Europe, the African troops took great comfort in re-creating their own indigenous religious practices, music, dance, war chants, and storytelling. It provided them a sense of continuity and security in otherwise dangerous and unfamiliar settings. The French, in contrast to the Germans, who carefully recorded and classified the languages and rituals of their African prisoners, tended to censor any African response to their situation. France wanted to maintain full narrative command over the lives of its colonial subjects, and might well have viewed indigenous practices as a form of resistance. France was also fearful lest the tirailleurs be exposed to radical ideas, especially by communists and Pan-Africanists, questioning colonialism itself and the French ideal of assimilation.[11] Postcard 7-14 then is rather unusual in presenting an image of tirailleurs sénégalais performing a native dance at a camp for tirailleurs in southern France. The caption on the back side of the card reads: "Tirailleur camp. Senegalese in the south of France: dances of their country." On the card's front, the same caption is inscribed in Arabic, a language rarely seen on cards depicting West African troops in Europe.

The French were well aware of the importance of employing colonial troops in their military and had a long tradition of doing so. In Fig. 7-15, a tirailleur holds his son in his arms above the caption: "Scenes and Types: a Future Tirailleur." "Scenes and Types" belongs to the many series of French cards that portray national, ethnic, and racial groups in an anonymous or stereotypical manner. Here the French are being reassured that a vast reserve of indigenous males remains to be exploited for deployment in present and future military campaigns. Indeed, in the 1920s, special schools (Écoles des Enfants de Troupe) were established for the sons of Senegalese soldiers, with priority given to children of WWI veterans. It was one of the few paths for the African soldiers to attain an officer's rank.

A semi-naked young African boy gazes at a tirailleur in full uniform who is striding confidently down the street (Fig. 7-16). The soldier, assimilated into the French military, stands as a model for progress and the future. Two other figures wrapped in traditional garments serve as contrast.

7009 SCÈNES ET TYPES. — UN FUTUR TIRAILLEUR.

Collection Idéale P S

Fig. 7-15

Fig. 7-16

Indigènes à Tombouctou (Soudan Français).

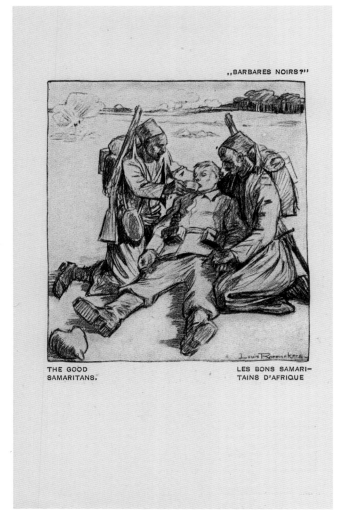

„BARBARES NOIRS?"

THE GOOD
SAMARITANS.

LES BONS SAMARI-
TAINS D'AFRIQUE

Fig. 7-17

21. GUERRE DE 1914 — Blessé allemand soigné par un turco   A. R.

Fig. 7-18

Postcards used in propaganda utilize the words "barbaric" and "savage" quite freely in describing the enemy. There are also cards that refute such accusations, such as the many produced in Germany picturing their soldiers giving food to French orphans. Because the African troops were at the center of so much of this controversy, it should come as little surprise that the French made a point of challenging German assumptions and defending the soldiers they viewed as products of their civilizing and assimilating mission.

A case in point is card 7-17, an illustration of two African tirailleurs coming to the aid of a wounded German soldier. In the upper right is the caption in quotes: "Black Barbarians?" Below left is written in English "The Good Samaritans" and across from it in French "The Good Samaritans of Africa." Fig. 7-18 is a photograph postcard sent by a French soldier who has just been returned to the trenches after a couple weeks behind the lines. It shows a black soldier kneeling beside a wounded German with the caption: "War of 1914 – A Wounded German cared for by a Turco."

Voilà ce que c'est qu'un sauvage.
That's what they call a savage.

Fig. 7-19

" Ti viens voir sauvages ? "
" You come to see savages ? "
„ Ты пришелъ посмотрѣть дикарей "

Visé Paris.
2058.
I. M. L.

D'après Jonas et l'Illustration.

Fig. 7-20

An ironic twist is given by two French cards designating the German and not the African as being the true "savage." A bilingual cartoon (Fig. 7-19) depicts a tirailleur pointing out a German prisoner to his girlfriend and explaining, "That's what they call a savage." The German looks down at the couple defiantly across the barbed wire. Interestingly, the tirailleur's admiring girlfriend is all but naked, a standard symbol for the unevolved African primitive. The caption is written in French and English.

In Fig. 7-20, a tirailleur sénégalais is standing guard over a number of captured German soldiers that a French family has come to view. The African, confident and relaxed, turns to the family and asks whether they have come to see the savages. The African is no longer the one being observed across a fence, as often happened at world's fairs and expositions. Now, it is the German who is the uncivilized one in need of guarding and the object of curiosity. The idea of a German being guarded by an African was particularly offensive to German sensibilities. Early in the war, Germany had complained that its prisoners were being shipped off to Africa, where they were being guarded by blacks and even tortured by them. The German government complained: "You French may consider the black race to be your equal, but we Germans put that race roughly on the level of apes."[12] The card's caption is written in petit-nègre, as well as in English and Russian.

The argument of who is really the civilized one and who the barbarian is humorously clarified by a tirailleur named Sidi to a sobbing German on card 7-21. The tirailleur explains in petit nègre: "I am the Negro, I am civilized, you are a Boche, you are barbaric, you are chocolate." The humor is multifold: a figure widely perceived as a savage is calling himself civilized while speaking a sub-standard French; a German soldier is so humiliated by charges of being barbaric he is reduced to tears; and in reversing commonly held stereotypes, the African inadvertently, perhaps having overly inculcated white racist norms, calls the German "chocolate," a pejorative term for "African." Sidi is a common name designation for an African (see Fig. 3-08).

Fig. 7-21

A more blatant attack on German Kultur is illustrated on card 7-22. It depicts an African tirailleur attacking a German soldier with his bayonet. The German, who has been thrown back helpless onto the ground, has a professorial look with his beard and spectacles. The African calls out: "ta KULTUR je m'en F.!" A translation might read "Your KULTUR/ I don't give a damn!" The German spelling of the word "Culture" is maintained, emphasizing the disdain it arouses in its pretense of being superior, while the uniformed African solider is barefooted, and thus all the more humiliating to the German.

Fig. 7-22

REPRESENTANTES DE LAS NACIONES ALIADAS QUE QUIEREN ANIQUILAR ALEMANIA Y AUSTRIA - HUNGRIA
CENTROS DE LA CULTURA Y DE LA CIVILIZACIÓN MODERNA

LOS REPRESENTANTES DE LA *CULTURA* Y DE LA *CIVILIZACION* CONTRA LOS *BARBAROS* ALEMANES Y AUSTRIACOS
ESCENA DEL CAMPO DE PRISIONEROS EN DÖBERITZ CERCA DE BERLÍN

Fig. 7-23

An illustrated Spanish card (Fig. 7-23) captures with irony the Allies' claims to be fighting a war for civilization against barbarism. Vividly pictured are a sampling of prisoners of war held by the Germans at their camp in Döberitz. Included are a group of North Africans at the lower right hunched over a meal, an Asian squatting opposite, and in the background an array of soldiers. These include a Scot made to look somewhat effeminate, a tirailleur sénégalais, French soldiers, Englishmen, an Asian Indian, and most absurdly, a barefoot African and a Native American, both in traditional dress. Some of the men are in communication, but the majority look lost and disgruntled. The captions are in Spanish. The upper one in red reads: "Representatives of the Allied Nations which want to annihilate Germany and Austria-Hungary/ Centers of modern culture and civilization." The caption below, in blue, reads: "Representatives of culture and civilization against the German and Austrian barbarians/ Scene from the prison camp at Döberitz near Berlin." With either reading, the disparate "races" are mocked as the embodiment of the less civilized.

Fig. 7-24 is an identical card, though this one is Italian and its one caption reads: "View of the nations in a concentration camp." It has been circulated as feldpost and bears a 1915 German postmark. Perhaps the censors preferred the distribution and circulation of this version of the card with its lackluster description over one whose caption ("Representatives of culture and civilization against the German and Austrian barbarians") might be interpreted literally by its users. The origin of the illustration on cards 7-23 and 7-24 is the German weekly humor magazine Lustige Blätter, where it is titled "Brothers in Culture in a P.O.W. Camp."

No better statement of the many ironies presented by WWI can be found on a single card than those appearing on Fig. 7-25. An Italian card depicts three colonial soldiers in the foreground—an Indian, a North African, and a tirailleur sénégalais. The Senegalese soldier points to a raging battle with charging soldiers, cannon fire, and burning structures in the background and, referring to the Europeans, remarks: "And to think it is they that taught us civilization!"

La Rivista delle Nazioni nel campo di concentrazione.

Fig. 7-24

E dire che sono quelli venuti ad insegnarci la civiltà!
Et dire qu'ils sont ceux qui nous ont appris la civilité!!

Fig. 7-25

NOTES

Introduction

1. Christaud Geary and Virginia-Lee Webb, eds., *Delivering Views: Distant Cultures in Early Postcards* (Washington: Smithsonian Institution Press, 1998), 42.

2. Annabelle Melzer, "Spectacles and Sexualities: The Mise-en-Scène of the Tirailleur Sénégalais on the Western Front, 1914-1920," in *Borderlines: Genders and Identities in War and Peace 1870-1930*, ed. Billie Melman (New York: Routledge, 1998), 238.

3. The title of the French military instructional pamphlet used to teach petit nègre was "Le Français tel que le parlent nos tirailleurs sénégalsais." ("The French as spoken by our Senegalese riflemen"). The Senegalese soldiers were well aware the "French" they were learning elicited ridicule from French when they spoke it. Lucie Cousturier, who has given us the most complete account of the experiences of a French civilian interfacing with the Senegalese soldiers and tutoring them in standard French in *Des inconnues chez moi* (*Strangers in My Home*) viewed petit nègre as a veritable "linguistic prison." See Brett A. Berliner, *Ambivalent Desire: The Exotic Black Other in Jazz-Age France* (Amherst: University of Massachusetts Press, 2000), 19–24.

Chapter 1

1. Joe Lunn, "Les Races Guerrieres: Racial Preconceptions in the French Military about West African Soldiers during the First World War," *Journal of Contemporary History* 34, no. 4 (October 1, 1999): 517–536.

2. Berliner, *Ambivalent Desire: The Exotic Black Other in Jazz-Age France*, 2.

3. Alongside the belief that non-Western peoples were trapped by biology and race in their inferiority and not particularly susceptible to environmental influences, some believed these same inferior peoples were capable, with European influence, of evolving to higher levels of civilization. This was the goal of France's mission civilisatrice. See Pascal Blanchard, Gilles Boëtsch, Nanette Jacomijn Snoep, eds., *Human Zoos: The Invention of the Savage* (Paris: Acts Sud and Musée du Quai Branly, 2011) for a well written and illustrated introduction to human zoos.

4. Nicolas Bancel, Pascal Blanchard, Gilles Boëtsch, et al., eds., *Zoos humains* (Paris: La Découverte, 2004), 15.

Chapter 2

1. Susan S. Hunter, *Black Death: AIDS in Africa* (New York: Palgrave Macmillan, 2003), 64.

2. Barbara Tuchman, *August 1914* (London: Constable, 1962), 522.

3. "Bloody Charge of the Turcos Troop," Stories from the Great War, 16 Dec. 2012, (Accessed 2 February 2015), http://storiesfromthegreatwar.blogspot.com/2012/12/bloody-charge-of-turcos-troops.html.

Chapter 3

1. Alison S. Fell, "Nursing the Other: the representation of colonial troops in French and British First World War nursing memoirs," in *Race, Empire and First World War Writing*, ed. Santanu Das (New York: Cambridge University Press, 2011), 163.

Chapter 4

1. Joe Lunn, *Memoirs of the Maelstrom: A Senegalese Oral History of the First World War* (Portsmouth, NH: Heinemann, 1999), 173.
2. For a fascinating account by a French officer about his relationship with tirailleurs sénégalais during the war and how his close contact with them resulted in his shedding many of his prejudices, see Nicole M. Zehfuss, "From Stereotype to Individual: World War I Experiences with Tirailleurs Sénégalais" in *French Colonial History*, 6 (2005), 137-158.
3. For an interesting discussion of the marraines, see Margaret H. Darrow, *Women and the First World War: War Stories of the Home Front* (New York: Bloomsbury Academic, 2000).

Chapter 5

1. Michel Verdenet, "Les Troupes Coloniales pendant la Grande Guerre," *Cartes Postales et Collection* 201 (Jan–Feb 2002) 14.
2. Annabelle Melzer, "Spectacles and Sexualities: The Mise-en-Scène of the Tirailleur Sénégalais on the Western Front, 1914-1920," in *Borderlines: Genders and Identities in War and Peace 1870–1930*, ed. Billie Melman (New York: Routledge, 1998), 231.
3. Melman, *Borderlines*, 231–233.
4. There is mention of incidents involving African tirailleurs beheading German soldiers and even carrying their heads in their rucksacks in Fischer and Dubois's *Sexual Life during the World War*, p. 443. Sources of the reports are the German periodical *Süddeutsche Monatshefte*, but also Robert Graves's *Good-Bye to All That*. It is perhaps noteworthy that the authors of *Sexual Life* refer to African troops generally as "barbarous" and "primitive," and place the discussion in a chapter titled "Sexual Perversions."
5. Tyler Stovall, *Paris Noir: African Americans in the City of Light* (New York: Houghton Mifflin, 1996), 19.
6. "EXPOMUSEUM: Exposition Universelle." http://www.expomuseum.com/1900/ (Accessed 21 January 2015).

Chapter 6

1. A similar attitude toward black soldiers being allowed to carry arms and possibly shooting white men was held by many in America's South when it came to arming African-American soldiers being sent to France in WWI. For a discussion of various parallels and contrasts in the experiences of African and African-American troops, see Tyler Stovall, *Paris Noir: African Americans in the City of Light* (Boston: Houghton Mifflin, 1996), 1–24.

2. BBC Media Centre, "Barbed Wire Ballads," (Accessed 21 January 2015), http://www.bbc.co.uk/mediacentre/proginfo/2013/11/barbed-wire-ballads.

3. Heather Jones, "Imperial captivities: colonial prisoners of war in Germany and the Ottoman empire, 1914–1918," in *Race, Empire and First World War Writing* (New York: Cambridge University Press, 2011), 179.

4. Uta Hinz, *Gefangen im Grossen Krieg. Kriegsgefangenschaft in Deutschland 1914–1921* (Essen: Klartext Verlag, 2006), 238.

5. Neger, a long-standing neutral term for black people, began to be viewed as derogatory beginning in the 1970s. *Schwarzer* (black person), *Farbiger* (colored person), or *Afrikaner* (African) are other commonly used terms, while *Mohr* (from Latin *morus,* black) is now obsolete, though it survives in advertising. See Ulrike Kramer, *Von Negerküssen und Mohrenköpften. Begriffe wie Neger und Mohr im Spiegel der Political Correctness – Eine Wortschatzanalyse* (Wien: Diplomarbeit, 2006), 84.

6. Jochen Oltmer, *Kriegsgefangene im Europa des Ersten Weltkriegs* (Paderborn: Schöningh, 2006), 71.

Chapter 7

1. Bakary Diallo was the only tirailleur sénégalais who published a memoir of his experiences in World War I. After being severely wounded, he learned French and wrote *Force-Bonté* in 1926. Roughly one hundred oral accounts exist of the tirailleur sénégalais experience, but these were mostly recorded over sixty years after the war's finish. See Berliner, *Ambivalent Desire: The Exotic Black Other in Jazz-Age France*, 28–30.

2. Berliner, *Ambivalent Desire*, 131.

3. "Germany," *Africana: The Encyclopedia of the African and African American Experience*, ed. Kwame Anthony Appiah and Henry Louis Gates, Jr. (New York: Basic Civita Books 1999), 827.

4. John Cornwell, *Hitler's Pope: The Secret History of Pius XII* (New York: Viking, 1999), 95.

5. In 1915 and 1916, widespread revolts occurred against conscription and French rule. See Myron Echenberg, *Colonial Conscripts: The Tirailleurs Sénégalais in French West Africa, 1857–1960* (Portsmouth, NH: Heinemann, 1991), 41–46.

6. Lunn, *Memoirs of the Maelstrom*, 135–6.

7. Léopold Sédar Senghor, *Poème liminaire,* (Accessed 1 March 2015), http://www.altersexualite.com/spip.php?article600.

8. Noel Barber, *The Week France Fell: June 1940* (New York: Stein and Day, 1976), 237.

9. Ibid.

10. Sally Marks, "The Myths of Reparations," *Central European History* 11, issue 3 (1978) 241.

11. Melman, *Borderlines*, 237.

12. Dick van Galen Last and Ralf Futselaar, *Black Shame: African Soldiers in Europe, 1914–1922* (New York: Bloomsbury, 2015), 162.

BIBLIOGRAPHY

Books

Bancel, Nicolas, Pascal Blanchard, Giles Boëtsch, et al., eds. *Zoos humains*. Paris: La Découverte, 2004.

Barber, Noel. *The Week France Fell*. New York: Stein and Day, 1976.

Berliner, Brett A. *The Exotic Black Other in Jazz-Age France*. Amherst, MA: University of Massachusetts Press, 2002.

Blanchard, Pascal, Giles Boëtsch, Nanette Jacomijn Snoep, eds., *Human Zoos: The Invention of the Savage* Paris: Acts Sud and Musée du Quai Branly, 2001

Bloom, Peter J. *French Colonial Documentary: Mythologies of Humanitarianism*. Minneapolis: University of Minnesota Press, 2008.

Cornwell, John. *Hitler's Pope: The Secret History of Pius XII*. New York: Viking, 1999.

Cousturier, Lucie. *Des inconnus chez moi*. Paris: L'Harmattan, 2001.

Darrow, Margaret H. *Women and the First World War: War Stories of the Home Front*. New York: Bloomsbury Academic, 2000.

Dornel, Laurent. *Les étrangers dans la Grande Guerre*. Paris: La documentation Française, 2014.

Echenberg, Myron. *Colonial Conscripts: The Tirailleurs Sénégalais in French West Africa, 1857–1960*. Portsmouth, NH: Heinemann, 1991.

Fargettas, Julien. *Les Tirailleurs Sénégalais: Les soldats noirs entre légendes et réalités 1939–1945*. Paris: Tallandier, 2012.

Fischer, H.C., and Dr. E.X. Dubois, *Sexual Life During the World War*. London: Francis Aldor, 1937.

Geary, Christaud, and Virginia-Lee Webb., eds. *Delivering Views: Distant Cultures in Early Postcards*. Washington: Smithsonian Institution Press, 1998.

Hinz, Uta. *Gefangen im Grossen Krieg. Kriegsgefangenschaft in Deutschland 1914–1921*. Essen: Klartext Verlag, 2006.

Hunter, Susan S. *Black Death: AIDS in Africa*. New York: Palgrave Macmillan, 2003.

Keen, Sam. *Faces of the Enemy: Reflections of the Hostile Imagination*. New York: Harper & Row, 1986.

Kramer, Ulrike. *Von Negerküssen und Mohrenköpften. Begriffe wie Neger und Mohr im Spiegel der Political Correctness – Eine Wortschatzanalyse*. Wien: Diplomarbeit, 2006.

Laffin, John. *World War I in Postcards*. UK: Wrens Park Publishing, 1988.

Last, Dick van Galen, and Ralf Futselaar. *Black Shame: African Soldiers in Europe, 1915–1922*. New York: Bloomsbury, 2015.

Lemaire, Sandrine, and Éric Deroo. *Histoire des Tirailleurs*. Paris: Éditions du Seuil, 2010.

Lunn, Joe. *Memoirs of the Maelstrom: A Senegalese Oral History of the First World War*. Portsmouth, NH: Heinemann, 1999.

Oltmer, Jochen. *Kriegsgefangene im Europa des Ersten Weltkriegs*. Paderborn: Schöningh, 2006.

Pieterse, Jan Nederveen. *White on Black: Images of Africa and Blacks in Western Popular Culture.* New Haven: Yale University Press, 1992.

Stovall, Tyler. *Paris Noir: African Americans in the City of Light.* Boston: Houghton Mifflin, 1996.

Tuchman, Barbara. *August 1914.* London: Constable, 1962.

Articles

Fell, Alison S. "Nursing the Other: the representation of colonial troops in French and British First World War nursing memoirs." In *Race, Empire and First World War Writing*, edited by Santanu Das, 158–74. New York: Cambridge University Press, 2011.

Ginio, Ruth. "French Officers, African Officers, and the Violent Image of African Colonial Soldiers." *Historical Reflections*, 36, no. 2 Summer 2010: 59–75.

Jones, Heather. "Imperial Captivities: colonial prisoners of war in Germany and the Ottoman empire, 1914–1918." In *Race, Empire and First World War Writing*, edited by Santanu Das, 175-93. New York: Cambridge University Press, 2011.

Koller, Christian. "The Recruitment of Colonial Troops in Africa and Asia and their Deployment in Europe during the First World War." *Immigrants & Minorities: Historical Studies in Ethnicity, minorities and Diaspora*, 26, issue 1–2 2008: 111–33.

Koller, Christian. "Representing Otherness: African, Indian and European soldiers' letters and memoirs." In *Race, Empire and First World War Writing*, edited by Santanu Das, 127–42. New York: Cambridge University Press, 2011.

Marks, Sally. "The Myths of Reparations," *Central European History*, 11, issue 3 1978: 241.

Melzer, Annabelle. "Spectacles and Sexualities: The 'Mise-en-Scène' of the 'Tirailleur Sénégalais' on the Western Front, 1914–1920." In *Borderlines: Genders and Identities in War and Peace 1870–1930*, edited by Billie Melman, 213–44. New York: Routledge, 1998.

de Perthuis, Bruno. "Le Soldat Noir et son Image pendant la Grande Guerre." *Cartes Postales et Collection*, 201 2002: 19–27.

Verdenet, Michel. "Les Troupes Coloniales pendant la Grande Guerre." *Cartes Postales et Collection*, 201 2002: 12–18.

Zehfuss, Nicole M. "From Stereotype to Individual: World War I Experiences with Tirailleurs Sénégalais." *French Colonial History*, 6 2005): 137–58.